The Paperback Mentor

ROBERT ROGERS

DEDICATION

Thank you God for giving me a life calling. It all belongs to you!

Thank you to my wife, Brittany, for your unwavering love and support. I got you!

To my kids, Logan, Tate and Leah. Thank you for helping me grow into a better Dad and person. I'm so proud you're mine!

Thank you to my brother Russell for making my vision a reality. I couldn't have done this without you.

Thank you to the United States Air Force. Joining the team almost two decades ago was the best decision of my life.

Finally, thanks to every person I've met and every experience I've had along the way. This book would not exist without you

CONTENTS

The Paperback Mentor

INTRODUCTION

Does anyone even read the intro section of a book anymore? I don't but for those who do, here you go! All you really need to know about me is I am an endeavoring Christian, striving Husband and imperfect Father of three; two buns from the oven and one off the shelf (my way of saying step-kid). I am also a disabled Veteran and Air Force Reserve Chief Master Sergeant who has faithfully served the United States of America for almost two decades in four separate military statuses (Active duty, Active Guard Reserve, Traditional Reservist and Individual Mobilization Augmentee). I have been through two divorces, prolonged physical ailments, a hair losing stress induced autoimmune disease called alopecia areata, loss of lives, depression, loneliness, suicidal thoughts, spiritual turmoil, long periods away from home, blended family situations, a boat load of crazy family scenarios and countless work related challenges. Throughout all of this, I have made mistakes, had several Aha moments, accumulated a decent amount of life experience and developed different ways of looking at things that I would like to share with you.

The intent of this book is to help you establish new habits, provide relatable experiences, make you think, give you new perspectives and learn practical concepts to apply in your everyday life. I do this by sharing my personal opinions, techniques, experiences and by asking questions, just as a mentor would in person. To communicate these objectives I will be using an informal, conversation like communication in the writing.

To be clear, just because I'm providing my unique viewpoint throughout this book, does not mean I think I'm right on everything. Just like you, my picture of the world has been painted by my successes, failures and experiences. If you disagree, that's ok. If you like, feel free to reach out and express your thoughts as well. I am always open to new opinions, insights or any constructive feedback you might have. My email address is provided at the end of the book.

Also, since I want you to finish this book I have intentionally kept it confined to fourteen chapters. For those checking it out from a library, my hope is you can finish a chapter each day and return the book before it's due. Additionally, since the average person reads at approximately 250 words per minute, each chapter is structured to take approximately 1% of your day to read.

That last sentence will make a lot more sense once you read the first chapter.

Furthermore, at the end of each chapter there will be a series of questions. To get the most out of this book, I recommend using a notepad to write down these questions and your unique answers. This step will allow you to explore your own personal experiences and develop new perspectives customized just for you. I am confident that by reading each chapter and answering the questions honestly, you will receive valuable insights to apply in your everyday life.

Finally, I'd like to take one moment to describe the cover art to you. This book is built around opening up my personal experiences with you, many of which came while serving our country. In the logo, the open book with five pages on each side signifies the bottom five stripes of the Air Force enlisted insignia. Many of the transformational experiences I've had were during that period of my career and I want to share them with you. The three blue colored arrows represent the top three enlisted ranks. Many Aha moments have come during this period and I've used these lessons to evolve and become a better leader. I hope you can too.

So without further ado, let's begin!

IT ALL STARTS WITH BALANCE

"Balance is not something you find, it's something you create." -Jana Kingsford

Have you ever seen someone who appears to have it all together? Their career is on the rise, family life seems amazing and they look like they can run a marathon without even training. Well experience has taught me these people aren't usually as put together as they seem. As humans, I believe we can sustain balance like this for a while but at some point reality will check us. For some, our bucket of cold water might be a promotion pass over, divorce, parenting challenge or too much time away from home. For others, it could be a physical injury affecting your quality of life and keeping you from the activities that help you stay centered. No matter the reason, life comes with challenges that knock us off course. So how do you get back on track? In this chapter, I will describe how I see balance, explain how I have failed to stay balanced and illustrate some methods I have developed to get back on track.

4

Balance

"Life is a balance between what we can control and what we cannot. I am learning to live between effort and surrender." -Danielle Orner

As far as I am concerned, living a truly balanced life is a myth, especially in the military. The demands of this profession aren't built for such a thing. Ask yourself if you've ever felt balanced while separated from your family, friends and routines. How about when you returned home and went through the process of reintegration with your unit and family? Something is always off. As I have sorted through my personal experiences, I have come to the conclusion that we are really only good at giving one or two key areas of lives the necessary effort required to make them fulfilling. This in turn creates a problem because when we're focused on those things, the other areas of our lives are slowly getting out of balance.

To give you a visual representation of how I see balance in our lives, I have divided life up into a three chamber hour glass (see illustration on next page). The sand inside each hourglass represents our time and our goal should be to keep each chamber equally full.

For me, the three chambers represent my **Career**, **Family** and **Self**! My goal is to keep each chamber equally full by regularly turning over the hourglass assembly. To do this effectively, I commit to giving time from the top chamber to fully focus on the areas being filled. In simpler terms, whatever I am focused on is on the bottom being filled with time from less emphasized areas on top.

Separated from home   **Return from travel**

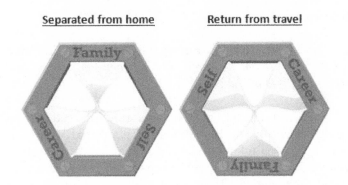

When traveling for work, my **Family** chamber begins to slowly drain but if I capitalize on this time away, I have a good opportunity to fill the **Career** and **Self** chambers of my life. When I get home, I start pouring sand back into my **Family** chamber and the **Career** and **Self** chambers start to slowly draw down. At times I have managed to turn the hour glasses over often enough to keep equal parts in each chamber, but over long periods of time this balance has proven to be unsustainable. However, what I have made peace with is giving my attention to the chamber being filled, so I can make significant strides in those areas and become more balanced overall.

The impact of multiple deployments

"Never get so busy making a living that you forget to make a life." -Dolly Parton

From 2011-2013, I left home on four deployments, one as a military member and three as a contractor supporting military operations. At the beginning of this stretch, I had a seven month old son and a stay at home spouse. In our view, these periods away from home were going to be great for my career, our pocketbook and as a bonus I would have some personal time to work on my physical fitness and goals.

Things started off well. Of course, there was an adjustment period for us all, but it was manageable as we all went through our new daily grinds. From my perspective, I was humming along performing operations and working to become an expert at my job. Naturally, I missed my family and they missed me but overall this first deployment went okay due to some awesome neighbors, a fiercely independent spouse and good fortune.

For us, the problems began when I came home. See, what I failed to realize during my time away was that my family established a new normal without me. Routines and ways of doing things were created in the void I left. When I came home, I changed all that. My thought upon returning was that I had to reintegrate as soon as possible. Additionally, I felt a need to unburden my spouse from all the duties she carried while I was gone. However, as good as my intentions were, these actions only led to frustrations for us all. After this first homecoming, it took a little while for me to get settled back into everyday life but eventually we were able to find our way and moved forward without any real issues.

Retrospectively, what I failed to take from the experiences of my first deployment were all the lessons I learned during the reintegration process. Furthermore, with each subsequent period away, my guilt and angst grew because I felt like I was abandoning my family. In turn, my desire to "fix" things when I got home grew stronger and stronger.

The second deployment was where things started to unravel. As I headed out the door again, this time as a contractor, I could feel my connection with home diminish a little. Just like the last time, I went out to do a mission I loved, had the freedom to do whatever I liked, was making more money than I knew what to do with and was only responsible for myself. Unfortunately, the inevitable hardships that come with travel and time away from home surfaced this time around. I remember vivid conversations about my son accidently hitting his face on a chair so hard that he developed a huge knot on his nose and black eyes. In another instance, my spouse tried to cut our son's hair and when it went wrong, she had to completely shave his head. I can still hear the anxiety in her voice as she described how poorly she felt she was doing as a mother and the despair I felt being on the other side of the world as she poured out her heart. I can recall the helplessness I felt knowing I could not relieve her and that when we hung up the phone, she would be on her own again.

Despite all of the challenges we faced during that second deployment, I still went out the door a third time. In my mind, it was my duty as a man to provide for our family and the struggles we would go through as a family would be worth the life I was determined to provide them. However, what I didn't realize at the time was that on this trip, my spouse began referring to herself as a single mother; and she was pretty much right. At that point I was simply a financial donor and it was on her to run the house, care for our son and take care of all of the responsibilities I left behind when I walked out the door. It was an unfair expectation for me to put on her as I continued to choose my own misguided intentions over the true well-being of our relationship and family.

Upon returning from this third trip, I felt like a stranger in my own home. I had come and gone so often that every daily, weekly or monthly routine was developed in my absence. Anytime I tried to interject, things only seemed to get worse. Furthermore, with the knowledge that I would be leaving again soon, it seemed senseless to interrupt their life so I learned to stay out of their way. In turn, I felt completely disconnected and became extremely depressed. As a result, I regularly turned to alcohol to numb my senses and desperately sought fleeting memory making moments that mimicked the connection I was seeking. In fact, at times I became so detached that I felt like a viewer passively watching my life on TV; like an on-looker viewing pivotal life events as they unfolded right in front of me.

By the fourth trip things were about as bad as they could be. We grew distant from each other, the daily chats were void of optimism, discussions of divorce were now a part of regular conversation and the connection with my toddler son was superficial at best. At this point, the time away from home felt more like a personal safeguard to delay the imminent moment of losing everything I loved. In my mind, my absence created a buffer to protect me from the inevitable negative consequences of my actions and knowing her heart, I knew I was fairly safe as long as I was gone.

This final trip ended up being my wakeup call to rejoin reality. Eventually, we were able to overcome these trials but it took a significant amount of time, mental health assistance for me and a new mindset to triumph over the challenges we endured over those three years.

To state the obvious, my life was out of balance. Although my **Career** and **Self** hourglass chambers were filled up nicely, my **Family** chamber was completely empty. I was so focused on making money and providing for my family that I refused to take time away from my **Career** and **Self** compartments to refill the chamber that held the most important people in my life. The funny thing is at the time, I believed I was doing a good job of balancing all three chambers. I thought I was providing opportunities for my family while having job satisfaction, but as I later found out, I was failing and had found myself in a situation that put me out of balance.

Taking Back 1%

"We cannot solve our problems with the same thinking we used when we created them" -Albert Einstein

As you saw in the last section, I allowed my life to get out of balance. Even after I made some big changes, I remained out of whack for some time and my next job didn't help matters. In my following job, I was submerged into one of the most poisonous work environments I have ever experienced. Every day was filled with so much stress, anxiety and job dissatisfaction that I developed an autoimmune disease called alopecia areata and eventually went bald. In fact, things got so bad that three members in our work center were on the verge of suicide, including me! We felt like everything we did was criticized, our careers were being sabotaged and we were marginalized amongst our coworkers. Out of sure survival, I knew I had to come up with something to get me back on track. That's when I developed the Taking Back 1% method.

Does 15 minutes sound like too much time for one personal need every day? It did to me! Who's got an extra 15 minutes? Well, I think you do and I will introduce you to a concept that I hope will change your perspective and show you how taking care of yourself is possible. I call it, Taking Back 1%.

In the course of life, we get so wrapped up in our careers, families and responsibilities that we forget to make time for ourselves. We run to work, pick up the kids, make dinner, clean the house, coach sports teams and before you know it the day is done and we're absolutely exhausted. After some significant struggles and a few years of doing this, I found that I was unhappy and stuck in a rut. I wasn't growing personally, my physical fitness was in decline and my mind was rarely being challenged. I considered ways to get myself back on track but was concerned that my actions might seem selfish. As I thought about the things I wanted to accomplish and goals I wanted to set, I realized that achieving them was within my reach but it would require me to change some habits.

My first personal goal was getting back into shape, so I committed to doing 30 minutes of cardio, 3 times a week. This seemed like an attainable goal to start with, it didn't required an unreasonable amount of time and when achieved, it would improve numerous aspects of my life; yet when I got home I found myself drained from work, busy with the night time routine and void of willpower. To state it simply, getting motivated to achieve a simple goal seemed a bridge too far, so I went back to the drawing board and set my sights on a lower, more realistic goal. That's when I had my Aha moment!

My initial thought was to focus 1% of my time each week on something just for me. Honestly, I choose this number because I expected the resulting time to be less than the 90 minute mark I was unable to hit, but as you'll soon realize this wasn't the case.

As I did the math I discovered that 1% of our week is about 100 minutes or 1 hour and 40 minutes; even more than the 90 minutes I was already failing to give to myself. *"I can't believe this!"* I thought, *"How am I not able to dedicate 1% of my own time to achieve a goal I'm saying is a priority in my life."*

If 100% of your time each day was equated to $1.00 would it be considered selfish to give away 0.99¢ and keep

0.01¢ for yourself? No, of course not!

To break it down farther, 1% of our day is 14.4 minutes. As I did some research on how I spent my time, I learned that on average I spent about 20 minutes a day getting ready for work, 23 minutes sitting at traffic lights, more time than I care to admit in the bathroom and almost 2% of my entire week was spent watching a single football game. These realizations were my catalyst to change. I realized then and there that I needed to make time for me. In that moment I pledged that everything else in my life can occupy the other 99% of my time but that 1% belonged to me and I am Taking It Back!

After this epiphany, I was determined to make full use of my 100 minutes a week. I started with a focus on physical fitness, specifically cardio. I kept a timer on my watch and every time I went running, I would hit start. Once it was over I hit stop. I did this all week, Monday thru Sunday, until I held myself accountable and saw that 1 hour 40 minute mark on my watch. When I met my physical fitness goals, I started applying this method to other aspects of my life.

My next goal was reading. The underlying motive for this goal came when I uncovered my hypocrisy. See, I had been telling my son that reading was super important and how much books can help you learn, yet I hadn't read a book that didn't involve a cat or a brown bear in at least five years. I knew I needed to spend some time challenging my mind and this habit would set a good example for my son, so I started using my 1% again. When I opened a book, I hit start on the timer and when finished, hit stop. Within a month I had finished my first real book in sometime. The next month I read another and the following month another. Once I established this habit, I actually started to enjoy reading and began learning more than ever.

Surprisingly, this new knowledge also enabled me to solve frustrating, ongoing challenges in my life. As I tell people now, *"You can't solve old problems with old knowledge. If you could, you would have by now. What you're lacking is knowledge and your solution can probably be found by learning something new."*

As I created these new patterns, learning became addictive! One easy change I made was streaming podcasts, TED Talks, sermons and speeches in the car to make better use of my commute time. Before then, most mornings were wasted listening to a song I'd heard a hundred times, celebrity gossip I cared nothing about or a pre-staged prank that had a predictable ending. Plus, none of these things got me closer to a goal, helped me learn or gave me a sense of satisfaction, so I changed the habit.

Taking back 1% has established transformational habits in my life. It has kept me on track for my health and focused on personal growth when I've gotten out of balance. Over the years, I have used my 1% to volunteer, learn new skills, prepare healthier meals and quietly meditate on life. If the ideas I previously listed don't spark something for you, Google search <u>15 minute habits</u> and you'll find over 79,000,000 results to kick start your mind.

By the way, there's more good news and the numbers become even more significant if you look at it over a one year period! Taking back your 1% equates to 5241 minutes a year, or about 87 hours. That's almost 4 full days each year you can take back to help you stay balanced. Maybe you can take a trip, find a new hobby, discover a passion, start a small business or finally chip away at some other postponed desire. Taking back 1% of your time can dramatically change your health, habits, mindset and life! I know this because it did for me.

So, say it out loud, *"I'm taking back 1%!"* I'm telling you, if you do this one simple thing, you will quickly see how your life improves and how the habits you develop will change your world for the better.

Doesn't it sound ridiculous to not give yourself back 1%? You're only asking to keep 0.01¢ from $1.00! So take it back from the rest of the world, don't negotiate with yourself and make that 1% count.

14.4 minutes per day = 100.8 minutes per week or 1 hour and 40 minutes

5241.6 minutes per year = about 87 hours a year or close to 4 full days

Waking up Early

"Lose an hour in the morning, and you will be all day hunting for it." -Richard Whately

So if you are anything like me, you'll find that even 14.4 minutes a day feels hard to come by. Furthermore, by the end of the day you're so exhausted that all you want to do is sit in silence, watch some TV, play games or just go to bed.

This feeling comes from your willpower being depleted throughout the day and I have used it as an excuse for not meeting my goals. Additionally, once I started looking at my old daily routine, I realized that there was zero room to get any of these so called "important" things done. That's when I came to the conclusion that I needed to do something radically different like; Wake up early! And not just a little bit earlier either. I'm talking about way before the kids get up so I can create more time than I need to simply eat and get ready for work.

For those of you who cringe at this idea, I assure you that this habit is not in my nature. I am usually the guy who wakes up at the last possible moment to scramble around and get things done in the nick time. Upon examination though, I found how this routine left my mornings feeling hurried. I noticed that if one of the kids wasn't moving at a pace I thought they should or if I hit even one hiccup on the way, frustration would set in and someone would inevitably be late for something. This kind of morning never put me in control of my day. Moreover, I never even had time to consider doing something for myself because I was constantly running from one thing to the next.

Then one day as I was using my commute time to fulfill my 1% goal of personal growth, I came across a message that changed my mind.

Waking Up at 4:00 AM Every Day Will Change Your Life

In this video, I heard about how the average millionaire wakes up at 4 A.M. The quotes and comments within sparked my curiosity! As I listened to other similar videos I learned that successful people use early morning hours to prepare for the day. Some work out, create mental clarity, meditate and even make big decisions. This sounded like all the things I wanted but never found the time to do. As I pondered this "radical" idea, I realized that getting things done before the kids woke up wouldn't take time away from my family and I could probably create a morning routine that didn't resemble a freshly kicked ant hill. So off I went setting various alarms, programming coffee makers, heading to bed early and mentally preparing myself for something I rarely and reluctantly did.

And guess what? It worked! Even the first morning was

pretty good! I got up, read my scriptures, got some coffee and sat down to write this book. The house was peaceful, the kiddos slept quietly and I slowly got into a groove to start knocking out things I wanted to achieve in my life. As time has gone on, waking up early has become a habit and I have been very satisfied with the quality of work I do in these early hours. Of course, some mornings don't always go as planned. Occasionally, one of the kids will hear me and come see what I'm doing or I decide to sleep in, but the habit is there and the results have been undeniable. So give it a try and I think you might find a better way to take on the day.

Question 1: What would be in your three hourglass chambers?

Question 2: What knocks you off balance?

Question 3: What's your trigger to know when you're off balance?

Question 4: What are you going to use your 1% on and why?

Question 5: How would waking up earlier make your day better or goals easier to achieve?

LIFE'S LEADERSHIP LESSONS

"If you had not suffered as you have, there would be no depth to you as a human being, no humility, no compassion." -Eckhart Tolle

If you've been on earth for any amount of time, you've probably encountered a few challenges. For some of us, adversity showed up in our childhood, others may not have experienced it until their perilous teenage years and for the remaining few, adulthood has probably introduced you to life's treasure trove of experiences. In fact, I've never met a person over thirty unscathed by the lessons of life. So, for those who have been through a few of these tough encounters, I have a question for you. Are you paying attention to the lessons in these moments or simply complaining about the ebbs of living? If you haven't yet been tested or tried, I hope you're preparing for the storms. Just as people prepare themselves for weather events, you can position yourself mentally, physically, spiritually, socially or financially to withstand a downpour before the clouds start to build. To shed a little more light on life's lessons, I will share some stories and personal truths I have learned up to now.

Stay Humble

"A teachable spirit and a humbleness to admit your ignorance or your mistake will save you a lot of pain. However, if you are a person who knows it all, then you have got a lot of heavy-hearted experiences coming your way." - Ron Carpenter Jr.

I have often found that humbling moments can be the most transformational events of our lives. Additionally, these events seem to find us at a point in our existence when we're capable of receiving them, even if we don't care much for the timing. Sometimes we are humbled by a miracle or success in the face of impossible odds. Other times we endure a gut wrenching defeat or encounter a challenge we've recently matured enough to face. My advice is to embrace these experiences. Both the good and bad contain knowledge. And no matter the outcome, remain humble through it all.

Has overconfidence ever gotten the best of you? It has me! One example came in my first marriage. I was so overconfident about our relationship that I failed to put the necessary work into it. I never looked at my shortfalls as a husband or sought to strengthen the weak points in our relationship. I just keep doing what I was doing without regard for the consequences. Then the moment came when she was reassigned to an overseas location for one year. I still remember sending her off with the belief that we'd get through this period and keep on truckin', but that wouldn't be the case. Within a month the phone calls got shorter and I could feel the distance widening. I scrambled to repair the relationship but four years of apathy had finally caught up with me. By the second month, she was already in the arms of another man and I found myself humbled. When I found out who she left me for, the gut check was debilitating. His personal life was a train wreck and his professional life was coming to an involuntary end. As I uncovered more about her new person, I came to realize that I had just been tossed aside for a clearly inferior guy. This ego demolishing, aggressively humbling moment was just one of many I've faced in my adult life.

However, after the storm cleared I realized there were some lessons in the experience. The main lesson was to never be arrogant about your statuses in life. Everything you claim has value needs time, energy and care. This can be applied to friendships, relationships, personal growth, etc... So don't take the important things for granted and if you care about something, give it effort with a humble heart.

Be Thankful

"Gratitude unlocks the fullness of life. It turns what we have into enough, and more. It turns denial into acceptance, chaos to order, confusion to clarity. It can turn a meal into a feast, a house into a home, a stranger into a friend." - Melody Beattie

Life is always better than we make it out to be. Of course, this is easier to see when you're not in the middle of a storm but I have learned to be thankful even when the rain is pouring down. Why? Because like a babbling brook slowing rounding a stone, life's rain has eroded my rough edges and shaped me into something different. This understanding has helped me become thankful for every person or experience I've had in my journey, because I've become a product of them all.

I have also come to realize that there are people in this

world who are happy with a lot less than you have, so be thankful for your health, finances and many other blessings. And be thankful for a living God who loves and cares for you, no matter where you go or what you do.

One thankful moment I can recall came when people were enraged about professional athletes kneeling during the national anthem. So many people were disgusted by their actions and expressed their strong patriotic opinions on the matter. Although I would never do this personally, when people asked me how I felt about it as a military member I replied, *"I'm glad they have the freedom to peacefully protest anything they want. Our duty as military members isn't to force patriotism on our citizens or judge those we don't agree with. It's to keep our freedoms safe from those who might try to infringe on our rights."* I have been to countries where a similar action would get you imprisoned or killed, yet here in America someone is free to take a knee and start a conversation. That is not a freedom we should take lightly and I am thankful our citizens have the right to peacefully exercise their freedoms however they see fit, regardless of how I feel about it.

Furthermore, if you live in America, you should be especially thankful for all the opportunities you have been presented. You have more access to information and resources than any other generation in the history of the world. You have the freedom to do what you want, or be what you want and to own every success or failure along the way. I recognize that we are not a perfect people but I can assure you from my experiences, the grass is not greener on the other side. Of the twenty or so countries I have been too, not a single one has come close to being as great as our United States of America. I am honored to serve our nation and thankful for the freedom and free will America affords us all.

Have Grace

"Make allowance for each other's faults, and forgive anyone who offends you. Remember, the Lord forgave you, so you must forgive others." -Colossians 3:13

We all make mistakes and the best leaders learn from them! In fact, they are usually better off for the lesson. So how can you overcome a personal bias against someone who acted recklessly five, ten or fifteen years ago? You extend them Grace!

All too often, I see people fall into the personal trap of thinking someone they knew in their twenties is still the same person in their thirties or even forties. During our early professional years, most of us go through life events that round our edges, teach us patience, empathy, humility and lend us new perspectives we've probably never considered. And as we have all experienced, change finds us with time, experience and maturity.

As an example, have you ever worked for a person without kids, a working spouse or some other significant responsibility in their personal life? It's like they can't comprehend why you are occasionally late or can't work the extended hours they do. In response, they may think you aren't planning well, getting up late or are just being lazy. Then one day life hits and they meet that special someone or have a significant life event that changes their world and they start rolling in late. In your mind, these people are the biggest hypocrites in the world. *How dare they!* This is the time you feel like giving them a piece of your mind but I would caution you against it. Why? Because in reality, these people are just starting to figure out what you knew all along and will soon learn the principles of understanding, empathy and grace.

My story of grace started as I was leaving a unit and decided to say something wildly inappropriate. My opinion at the time was that the work culture allowed for this type of comment and I thought the expression was humorous and shocking enough to leave a lasting impression. Well as I am sure you can guess, this moment garnered a mixed response. Some folks smiled while others gasped. The look from the gaspers made it clear they were offended. Shortly thereafter my leadership team took me aside to have a talk with me. They explained their dissatisfaction but since I was leaving, there wasn't much they could do.

Personally, I was indifferent about the situation because I believed I was leaving this place and never coming back. Fast forward two and a half years and an opportunity arose to go back to the same area but not the same unit. As I looked into the opportunity, I discovered that the Commander of the Squadron I wanted to join was in the room when I made the inappropriate comment. Better yet, the second in charge was there too. EEssh! I honestly considered not applying because I was sure they would never hire someone who just two years ago decided saying something offensive was acceptable. Eventually, I got up the courage to apply and during the interview I had to explain and atone for my previous actions. This left me feeling uneasy about the interview and unconfident about my prospects. However, these two people extended me grace and despite my reputation, hired me into a leadership position. They expressed to me that I was not defined by a single action and how they believed I had learned a lesson, expressed genuine remorse and was the right person for the job. I could not have been more grateful and worked every day to regain their trust and repay my gratitude for their grace based decision.

My point is, sometimes you're on the giving side and

sometimes you're on the getting side of grace. This one act of kindness changed my views on grace and forgiveness. I no longer hold grudges for ten year old insults or maintain opinions about someone from my adolescent years. I give grace because I know what it's like to receive it. If you're holding onto something, I would encourage you to forgive and give grace. Why? Because I have found that forgiveness and grace are the keys that free us from the shackles of anger and past transgressions.

Listen through gossip and rumors

"Be quick to listen, slow to speak and slow to get angry"
-James 1:19

As a leader, how do you handle gossip and rumors in your organization? Do you tell people to knock it off, keep spreading the dirt or have you considered listening through the gossip to understand the underlying issue? I know this may sound a bit different, but hear me out. What does almost every gossip or rumor have in it? A person in transition! And what is a person in transition likely experiencing? Stress!

When I hear a rumor, I seek to understand its truth and potential outcomes. For example, if a rumor is going around about a member cheating on their spouse, I wonder if there might be domestic concerns, broken family issues, financial complications, mental health troubles, child welfare problems, etc... Then at an appropriate time, I approach the central person with an open heart and non-judgmental mind to discuss the validity of these stories. If true, I listen to the situation and work to get them the resources both they and their family may need. If false, I search for the source and inquire about the cause.

If I hear gossip about a single young woman becoming

pregnant, I work to find out what her support network is like, if she's in a good relationship, if she may need financial assistance or if she just needs someone to lend a caring ear. If this story is true, her life's going to change radically and she'll need a team around her building her up, not tearing her down.

I am slow to get angry or shut down these channels of communication, because sometimes they are the only way I learn about issues afflicting my people. If I tell people to knock it off, I may discover these issues too late or not at all. If I spread them, I'm doing more harm than good. But if I listen and act on the behalf of the central person, I have a chance to intervene when things are still manageable. Of course, I don't condone this type of behavior and I always encourage people to come talk to me if they have an issue but you need to be realistic as a leader. Gossip and rumors will always exist. They're as old as time. Either you can be in the know or attempt to shut them down and get cut out of the loop.

No comments before context

"It is better to bite your tongue than eat your words."-Frank Sonnenberg

Have you ever made a snarky comment about something before you knew the whole story behind it? I have several times but when it happened to me, it opened up my eyes to a whole new perspective.

In my case, I was running late to a seminar due to a sick family at home. After seeing the bodily carnage that morning, I decided running late was worth making sure I left the house in decent condition; so I took a little extra time to clean up their messes before I pressed on with my day. This delay caused me to arrive about ten minutes late and as I quietly tried to sneak in thru the back door, I heard someone say, "*I guess we can show up whenever we want!*"

Now don't get me wrong, before this moment I would have absolutely said something like that. However, today was different because I had context. Just then, I looked over and realized that the person firing off this callous comment was a First Sergeant. In the military, a First Sergeant's main job is the health of an organization and wellbeing of its people.

At first, I let the comment slide but as time went on, something irked me about our interaction. See, what this person didn't know was how my morning was going or how I left two people I cared about sick at home. She had no clue that I was cleaning up vomit all morning. She didn't understand why I made the decision to be late and just assumed I was a dirt bag.

At the next break, I decided to go talk with her. I explained what my morning was like and how this comment was unwarranted. I went on to remind her that someone in her position should remain approachable and how a comment like this would have shut down communication with almost any other person. In return, she apologized and made general statements about her experiences with late people, which I understood. My hope was in the future she'd talk to people before passing judgement and in that moment, I realized this advice was good medicine for me as well.

The next time you see someone coming in late or doing something out of character, reserve your smart mouthed comments. They never help and you typically end up alienating a person who might actually need your assistance. If you have concerns, talk with the individual and find out what's causing this behavior. If it's a one off mistake, address it as required. But if it's a manifestation of a bigger issue, be the support network that helps them through, not the person who shuts them down.

Just be human sometimes

"Do not let the roles you play in life make you forget that you are human." -Roy T. Bennett

I feel like people get so caught up in their positions that sometimes they forget how to be human to a person dealing with real problems. In response to an issue, they express their concerns with muted emotions or military tact; yet the person being affected may just need a cup of coffee and a sympathetic ear.

When someone is struggling at home, offer them a night of babysitting so they can reconnect with their spouse or get a good night's sleep. If they are going through some personal struggles, share some of your vulnerabilities with them and what things look like on the other side. If you can't relate, introduce them to people who can, ask around or find them resources. At the end of the day, we're all people. So, don't be afraid to remove your mask and connect with people at the human level. I believe it's one of the most authentic leadership traits a person can have.

Hear or gone

"Leaders who do not listen will eventually be surrounded by people who have nothing to say." -Andy Stanley

Do you feel like you are being heard at work? If not, how many times have you voiced your concerns without resolution or feedback? Now how likely are you to voice them again?

As leaders, we must make time to listen to our people. This is one of the main ways we can make improvements in our work centers and garner buy in from our teams. I have probably had a dozen leaders in my career that acted like they were genuinely interested in my concerns, only to find out they thought I was lying, blowing things out of proportion or just delusional. Honestly, I would rather have a leader not ask for my inputs, than to ask and ignore my concerns. So if you are going to ask for feedback and then dismiss it when it's not what you want to hear, don't even ask. I get how perspectives change once you move through higher management levels and how sometimes your folks concerns may not be as bad as they think. However, remember that their perception is someone's reality and their inputs can be very valuable in solving underlying issues. From personal experiences, I can tell you that if you don't listen to your people, they will stop talking. I have seen this play out time after time and it has always resulted in frustrated leadership teams, disgruntled employees and toxic work environments. In one case, I saw an organizational collapse and mass exodus of people because things got so bad. Although many factors were at play in that situation, I believe the main reason for this exodus was the work force felt like they weren't being heard. In turn, they lost hope that things would improve and chose to leave.

So don't be this kind of leader. Ask your people for feedback, stay open to their inputs and genuinely care for the concerns they express no matter how trivial you may feel they are.

A sword is formed in the fire

Think of your life and leadership skills starting off like a chunk of metal. In the beginning, it doesn't have any real shape and can be anything you want. However, in order to make that chunk of metal into something noteworthy, you need to have some kind of plan for it. In this case, our plan is to turn this metal into a sword. In life, you need to figure out what you are and create a plan to get there.

Once you have decided the metal will become a sword, you should spend some time reading, learning and asking questions about sword making. Just heating and hammering metal won't make it into a sword. You have to approach this endeavor with some skills and knowledge to increase your likelihood of success. In life, this is where you put in work through self-discovery, reading, learning or finding a mentor before the heat is applied.

The next step is applying heat to the metal. Heat expands metal and prepares it for change. Without heat, changing the shape of metal is hard. And if you do find some way to change the shape without heat, chances are the metal will remain too brittle to become a high quality sword. In life, heat comes in the form of humbling situations, difficult subordinates, terrible bosses, personal hardships or significant setbacks. These experiences are not easy but if you let them, they will expand your mind and shape you into something different. When you find yourself in the fire, remember that it's helping you change.

After sufficiently heating the metal, you will need to consistently hammer and patiently shape it into the form you want. Consistent actions are key to shaping you into the person you want to be. If you only hammer the metal once or twice, you won't make a sword. You must hammer it thousands of times with deliberate strikes to create your vision.

Cooling the metal is a crucial step in the sword making process. Tempering metal decreases hardness, decreases brittleness and makes the metal tougher. In life, take a moment after the fire to reflect on your experiences, develop empathy and increase your resiliency. Taking time to step away from the heat prepares you for the next time you are put in the fire.

Finally, after you have learned, honed your skills, gone through the fire, been hammered into shape and grown tougher through the process, you will look and feel like a sword. However, the final step to becoming a sword is having a sharp edge. If you go through all those steps and never gain an edge, you will never be an effective sword. In life, you can maintain your edge by constantly learning, applying your skills and serving those around you. However, if you use your sword enough, you will probably end up with a dull blade. In life, take time to restore your edge, apply your 1% to sharpening the blade and remain ready to cut through challenges when the time comes.

Take away

No one succeeds without other people's help. We all need someone to give us a break, mentor us, support us financially or pick up our slack. To think you can be successful without someone else's assistance is naïve. Recognize all of the contributions others have made in your life. Even the negative experiences are contributing to your success and propelling you to greatness. In fact, those hard times might be the most valuable. So the next time you are shaking a hand or receiving an accolade, stay humble and remember that your success did not come in spite of your experiences; it came because of them.

Question 1: What experience has humbled you?

Question 2: What are you thankful for?

Question 3: Who can you extend grace to?

Question 4: How do you handle rumors and gossip?

Question 5: Have you ever received a comment from someone who didn't know all the facts? How'd you feel?

Question 6: What situation in your life could use a human touch?

Question 7: What was the heat that helped form you?

Question 8: How are you staying sharp?

HOW LOW PERFORMERS ARE HELPING YOU SUCCEED

"Think of difficult people as sandpaper. They may rub you and scratch you painfully but eventually you end up smooth and the sandpaper worn out." -Raymund Salumbides

Have you ever observed or supervised a person who never met expectations? They're constantly late, miss deadlines, have issues outside of work or simply fail to transition their language and behaviors for a professional environment. As frustrating as these people are, they serve a crucial role on your path to becoming a leader. In fact, I would say their actions create more acumen within you than any book or advice can provide. Why? Because they are making their problems, your problems! This association forces you to take personal ownership of their issues, which stimulates change within you. When you learn how to handle an infuriating moment without yelling, a change occurs. When you discover the importance of controlling your emotions, compiling your thoughts and executing effective messaging in the face of lies, deception or flaring tempers, a change occurs. Advice and books are great but there is no substitute for feeling an emotion and handling the situation appropriately. If you want to be a well-rounded leader, take on the low performers, recognize their value and embrace the challenge.

My first low performer

"Sometimes those who challenge you the most teach you best." -Anonymous

My first low performer surfaced about five years into my military career. Before him, antics and irresponsible behaviors seemed like fun. However, once I became accountable for his actions, my perspective changed. He was a genuinely nice guy but made terrible decisions and for some reason could not get out of his own way. In the year or so I supervised him, he had two alcohol related incidents, was consistently late, could not accomplish simple training requirements and so on. Oh, and of course no matter what the situation was, someone else was to blame.

One impactful moment with him came right before an alcohol treatment meeting with our Commander and First Sergeant. To make a good impression I only asked two simple things of him. Show up on time and look sharp. That's it! Instead, he showed up about ten minutes late, sprinting up the stairs out of breathe, looking like he'd just changed the oil in his car. As I stared a hole through him, I had to keep my emotions in check and address these maddening issues after the meeting was over and our leadership team departed.

Another time, he claimed that while out at the club, some guy came out of nowhere to punch him in the face and kick him in the head. For no reason! As we talked through this encounter I explained to him that his story didn't seem to add up. As a matter of fact, it all sounded pretty personal to me. Defiantly he stuck to his narrative. However, upon further investigation I discovered that he was dating a girl with several local romantic interests, he became incredibly belligerent when drinking and that his intoxicated dance style belonged in a mosh pit, not a nightclub. Of course, this enlightening information was easily uncovered by simply talking with people in his social group. And although I never found the root cause of his club incident, it seemed like any of these things could have been reason enough. The lesson from this incident was to listen with intent, be patient and gather the facts before taking action.

This guy was just one of at least ten legitimate low performers I have personally interacted with in my professional life. With each new person, unique challenges are brought to my doorstep. In response, I have learned how to navigate these trials and extract the imbedded lessons. As a result, my career, leadership style and personal growth have matured and I have become better through the experiences.

How low performers help you succeed

"Dealing with employee issues can be difficult, but not dealing with them can be worse." -Paul Foster

Low performers are valuable to your personal growth story. For starters, they offer you a variety of situations you would probably never face if you only had superstars on your team. Additionally, they force you into uncomfortable positions, challenge your patience and push you out of your comfort zone. You may not like the circumstances they create but if you look at these moments as learning opportunities, keep an open mind, seek to understand and educate yourself about the problems they present, you will come out as a better leader every time.

Here are some specific ways low performers help you succeed.

1. They challenge you as a leader.

Low performers force you to develop new leadership tools and find different solutions. Each low performing individual has a unique set of circumstances producing their behaviors. As you learn about the roadblocks in their life, such as bad habits, bad relationships, negative mindsets, etc..., you will need to provide insight or recall personal experiences to help them see a better path. Low performers have forced me out of leadership ruts and pushed me to step up my game. Because of the challenges they have presented, I've had to read more, listen harder, ask more questions and try unfamiliar techniques in an attempt to reach them where they are. Once I find our connection point, I can work on raising them up. As a bonus, sometimes this research and discovery process reveals deficiencies in my own disposition, prompting me to make incremental improvements within myself.

2. They force you to learn about the rules, policies and regulations of your organization.

How often are you internally motivated to research the rules, policies and regulations of your organization? Well, low performers provide an external motivation that helps you better understand your organization. They press you to figure out proper documentation for their behaviors, what specific rules or regulations to annotate and how to levy the appropriate corporate corrective actions. If they mess up often enough, you might even become the go-to person for these processes. And if you're really fortunate like I was, you might get so good at this stuff that the knowledge gained will earn you an extra twelve points on a promotion test, directly contributing to your career advancement.

3. They provoke difficult conversations.

When you have a low performer, at some point you will probably need to have a difficult conversation. In these moments you might have to give direct feedback, speak an uncomfortable truth, hit on a sensitive topic or simply explain the purpose for letting them go. These are never easy conversations but are necessary if you want to call yourself a leader. Like it or not, this group of people push you to practice the critical art of difficult and effective communication.

4. They help you develop relationships.

Often times with low performers you find yourself reaching out to others for advice. This could be a manager, mentor or coworker that has relatable experiences. When you do this, you create opportunities to build meaningful relationships. With a common connection point, you can create a foundation on which to build rapport and establish a lasting bond. In turn, these relationships can provide opportunities to progress in your professional career or reveal some unknown leadership opportunities. In fact, issues prompted by your low perform might just be the opening you need to develop a key relationship.

5. You learn enough to be helpful to others.

Since low performers compel you to learn and grow, they might be increasing your value to others. When you think of someone in your professional life you admire, do you consider how they gained their wisdom? Do you think they learned everything from a book? Why do you think they can confidently give advice on your issue? My guess is because they have probably experienced challenging people, difficult situations or unique moments that gave them their perspective. Over time, their tough encounters became the wisdom they share with you today.

Why A, B, C, D, and F students matter

Employers are always seeking those few superstar employees who can hit the ground running. High speed, low drag! But realistically, only so many of these people exist in the world. A majority of the time you just need a butt in the seat. This reality means you might need to look at a person who isn't up to your standards or needs some work to realize their potential. This is where your role as a leader comes in. It is your job to get these low performers operating at an appropriate level for their assigned tasks. If you approach this challenge with an open mind, you can integrate these people into your team, develop them within your organization and increase your skills as a leader.

Here's how I breakdown people at work, their pros, cons and what they may need from you.

A Student-

Pros- Does great work, always up to the challenge, exceeds expectations and is highly reliable. They challenge you in positive ways. You may need to grow and learn as a leader to assist in their development. They almost always have a sharp edge or two you can work on.

Cons- May be high maintenance at times, require additional work for recognition programs and inadvertently ask lots of time consuming questions. Many seem to desire one on one time to feel valued. At times, they have a tendency to take on more than they can handle and have a hard time saying no. Their performance can make other members of a team feel inadequate or insignificant.

Conclusion- This person is worth the extra work. Do your best to help them grow in areas they are weak and be active in their development. Also, do not let them get overtasked or burnt out due to their internal drive. Groom these people to step in when you move on to your next position.

B Student-

Pros- Does good work and is a team player. Little to no drama. Will do everything they are told to the best of their ability and gives a little extra at times.

Cons- Will likely meet but not exceed your expectations. Rarely pushes their personal growth or strives for leadership roles. Content with support roles and prepared to assist, during defined work hours.

Conclusion- Probably your most low maintenance person. This person can easily become an A student if they want too. They are your worker bees who complete daily tasks and keep the organization running smoothly.

C Student-

Pros- They get the job done but may need someone holding them accountable along the way. They possess the ability to step up their game but often don't have the knowledge or drive to make that leap. People in this group have potential.

Cons- They tend to be misunderstood and might have some personal issues interfering with their professional life. They tend to carry one or two major flaws such as being a manipulator, gossip, narcissistic or overly crass. It is easier for them to go down than up.

Conclusion- This group needs an active leader in their life giving them direction, guidance and feedback. They may have the skills to do better but their misperceptions, poor attitude or lack of knowledge might be holding them back. Don't let them slip down a grade. Provide the necessary effort to enhance their performance.

D Student-

Pros- Typically seem to care and remain open to making changes for the better, if you can make it real for them.

Cons- They can't seem to get out of their own way and can be frustrating at times. Many of their mistakes are due to poor choices and a reluctance to change the behaviors that have kept them down.

Conclusion- Your greatest satisfaction as a leader can come from this group. There are diamonds in the rough but you will have to dig them out. If you want to be impactful, you need to find out what motivates them and press the right buttons. They will push you as a leader and can kick start substantial growth in your own personal development.

F Student-

Pros- If you are going to call yourself a leader, these are the people you must confront. Lots of opportunities for you here!

Cons- This group can be toxic in a work center. They generally don't care, complain non-stop and create negative environments. They have no intent to join the team or contribute to the collective goal.

Conclusion- These are the people you may need to let go. Sometimes people don't want to change and it's no longer a good fit for them and your organization. If this is the case, help them on their way and start over with someone new.

Overall, I would categorize my first low performer as a D student. Although he made a lot of mistakes, he actually maintained a decent attitude. The list went on with him, but I am thankful for the experience he gave me. Before him, I never understood how to profit from a low performer. Now I see the value.

Lastly, if you want to see what your superstar employee is made of and how they perform as a leader, give them a D student. Sure a superstar supervising another high performer is great for the subordinate, but it's probably not all that challenging for the superstar. So if you want to uncover a high performing supervisors' leadership shortfalls and encourage growth, give them a challenge and let them develop through experience.

Does a little change matter?

"If you do not change direction, you may end up where you are heading." -Lao Tzu

Would nudging your low performer in the right direction really make a difference? Is a little growth worth your effort? As human beings, I think we forget how small changes impact us. To believe an impactful moment has occurred, we look for an immediate change instead of a gradual improvement. However, the true impact of a small change can reveal itself, if you just give it time. To put things into perspective, I will illustrate how small changes in our everyday lives can make a big difference.

In climate, world leaders and scientists have proclaimed that a two degree Celsius rise in global temperature would cause massive weather pattern changes, rising sea levels and the elimination of some species. As a result, it is predicted that fresh water resources will diminish, food supplies will be impacted and large migrations of people will take place. For many of us, we wouldn't even notice a two degree change in our homes, yet if it occurred at a global scale we would all feel the effects.

Space is another area where two degrees matter. If you have satellite TV and get hit by a big storm you might lose your signal. If this occurs you may need to repoint your dish. This isn't a particularly hard task but if you are off by even a small amount, it makes a huge difference. That's because little pointing changes on the Earth have huge effects in space. Even something small like a two degree change in your pointing angle occurs with little more than a nudge of the dish. However 22,300 miles away where the satellite is orbiting, your two degree nudge has pointed you almost 800 miles off target. Once again, that small change may not be noticeable up close but it makes a big difference down the road.

As a final example, people investing for retirement may not view two percent as a significant amount to their portfolio. However, the following scenario will show just how impactful it can be.

In this case a 25 year old made an initial investment of $10,000 and contributed $250 a month until they reached 65.

So what's the difference between a 6% return and 8% over those 40 years?

At 6% the portfolio value would be $607,447.

At 8% it would be $1,115,485.

That's an extra $508,038 from a paltry two percent difference each year. Who would have thought that small amount could put you in the millionaire's club?

So how does this concept apply to our people? We are all heading somewhere in life, right. Some know where they're going while others need a little nudge in the right direction. By giving constructive feedback or advice, you can initiate a change to set your people on a new path. Take a second to consider how revealing an undesirable trait can have a positive long-term impact on a young professional. How a slight shift in thinking can move someone a couple degrees in the right direction. How a small nudge can change the course of someone's life; or how investing a little extra time into someone can pay huge dividends in their life.

So you tell me, *"Does a little change matter?"*

Two quick pieces of advice

First, when a person makes a mistake my first inclination is they lack the knowledge to make a correct decision or execute an appropriate action. Once I ensure training and education has been provided, I hold them to a higher standard. In the meantime, I refrain from disciplining people for mistakes due to ignorance.

If they have received education on an issue, I ensure they get remedial training, direct them to take notes, document the training in their records and ask if there are any areas they still have questions on before returning to their duties. These specific actions communicate to them that from here on out, they are accountable for doing their job correctly and if they have questions, they should refer to their notes or ask questions before taking action. Once these measures are completed, I feel justified in any appropriate actions to correct their behaviors.

Second, when a person does something foolish my first question is, *"What was your intent behind that action?"* Often times I have found that a person's intentions are good but their methods are bad. If you understand what someone is trying to accomplish, you can help them be more effective in achieving their intended goal. Additionally, you create an opportunity to provide mentorship that may keep them from making the same mistakes in the future.

It's all just a puzzle

Think of a low performer as a puzzle you must solve. When presented with a puzzle, what's the first thing you do? My first step is to take time to look it over, analyze the different components and devise an initial best approach to solving it.

When your initial approach doesn't work, what's your next step? You try a bunch of other methods and ideas to see if any of them work.

If that fails, what might you do? I ask friends or colleagues for some pointers to help me solve it.

If they can't help you, what's your last move? If you're like me, I would search the internet, find possible solutions and enact that knowledge to solve my problem.

So how are these steps to solve a puzzle any different than solving the enigma a low performer presents you?

Evaluations of the disciples

On the next page is a story I've heard a few times, and it reminds me of the impact so called low performers can have on the world. I think it captures what modern day talent evaluators would have thought of Jesus's chosen disciples and how genuine leadership can change a bunch of low performers into world changing figures. Additionally, there's a surprise twist at the end that reminds me to take outside opinions with a grain of salt. Enjoy!

To: Jesus, Son of Joseph
Woodcrafter's Carpenter Shop
Nazareth 25922
From: Jordan Management Consultants

Dear Sir:

Thank you for submitting the resumes of the twelve men you have picked for managerial positions in your new organization. All of them have now taken our battery of tests; and we have not only run the results through our computer, but also arranged personal interviews for each of them with our psychologist and vocational aptitude consultant.

The profiles of all tests are included, and you will want to study each of them carefully.

As part of our service, we make some general comments for your guidance, much as an auditor will include some general statements. This is given as a result of staff consultation, and comes without any additional fee.

It is the staff opinion that most of your nominees are lacking in background, education and vocational aptitude for the type of enterprise you are undertaking. They do not have the team concept. We would recommend that you continue your search for persons of experience in managerial ability and proven capability.

Simon Peter is emotionally unstable and given to fits of temper.

Andrew has absolutely no qualities of leadership.

The two brothers, James and John, the sons of Zebedee, place personal interest above company loyalty.

Thomas demonstrates a questioning attitude that would tend to undermine morale.

We feel that it is our duty to tell you that Matthew had been blacklisted by the Greater Jerusalem Better Business Bureau.

James, the son of Alphaeus, and Thaddaeus definitely have radical leanings, and they both registered a high score on the manic-depressive scale.

One of the candidates, however, shows great potential. He is a man of ability and resourcefulness, meets people well, has a keen business mind, and has contacts in high places. He is highly motivated, ambitious, and responsible. We recommend Judas Iscariot as your controller and right-hand man. All of the other profiles are self-explanatory.

Sincerely,

Jordan Management Consultants

For those who may not know, Judas was the man that betrayed Jesus. Conversely, Jesus did not focus on the negative traits of his other disciples but instead had a vision of what they could become. As a leader, Jesus smoothed out their rough edges and helped them reach their true potential. When you look around your work center, do you see the potential in people or make assumptions based on the opinions of others?

Question 1: Who is the low performer you remember most?

Question 2: How are you better off now for that experience?

Question 3: What type of student are you?

Question 4: Are you correcting people without knowing all the facts? Do you know their intent?

Question 5: What positives can you think of for your low performer? How can you capitalize on their strengths?

Question 6: What small change can you initiate to set your low performer on a better path?

GET OUT OF YOUR COMFORT ZONE

"Life begins at the end of your comfort zone." -Neale Walsch

I believe personal growth exists in higher concentrations outside of our comfort zones. I also believe there are things we CAN do and things we CHOOSE to do. For instance, if you know your calling in life and choose to stay in an unfulfilling job, that's a choice. If you are in a relationship that doesn't bring you joy or has no value, that's a choice as well. And in the eternal words of the band Rush, *"If you choose not to decide, you still have made a choice."* Leaving your comfort zone is a <u>choice</u> and if you want to be more than you are right now, you will have to leave what's comfortable and take a journey into the unknown.

Just think about what your life could be if you gave it everything you got!

The Zones

"You are only confined by the walls you build yourself."
-Andrew Murphy

Getting out of your comfort zone can be a daunting task and when you leave it, where do you go? To guide you into more enriching areas of life, I have created a concept to show you a way.

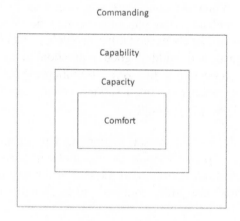

Comfort zone- This zone requires nothing new or challenging from you. When you operate here, your life tends to be very predictable. Since you are not doing anything to advance yourself, career, finances or family life, chances are everything will fall into place as expected. When someone sees you operating in the comfort zone, they will probably view you as an average person doing good work. In this state, you will consistently meet expectations but internally you will know you could be doing more. Most people live in the comfort zone because it's safe and opportunities for risk or disappointment are few.

Visually, I see people in the comfort zone as floating on a lazy river. No effort required and no fear or adventure.

Capacity zone- This zone is where the best version of your current self exists. It's where you take all the knowledge and skills you have accumulated over the years and apply it to your everyday life. In this zone, you are not deliberately looking to learn something new, although you might stumble onto something occasionally. You are just doing what you already know at the highest possible level you can. When someone sees you operating in this zone, they will probably view you as someone who goes the extra mile. You will likely exceed other people's expectations on a regular basis and build a good reputation in the process. People who operate in this zone are noticeable because they deliver outstanding customer service, enhance an experience or present exceptional value.

Visually, I see a person swimming laps in an Olympic sized pool. To non-swimmers, this looks impressive and a little exhausting. However, at the end of the day their skills and efforts are still confined to a small, controlled environment.

Capability zone- This zone is where you push out from your perceived limits and start trying to reach your true potential. To get there, you have to build good habits such as reading, learning and humility to grow. In this zone you accept that you don't know everything and listen to the people around you with a curious spirit. You may also have to address some weaknesses or reveal vulnerabilities at times. This zone can be uncomfortable at first and remaining here requires effort. When people see you operating in the capability zone, they might think you're going places in life. They might also be drawn to your curiosity or growth mindset. People operating in this zone might be seen quickly moving through the ranks of a company or receiving recurring notoriety.

Visually, I see someone operating in the capability zone as a person saving someone in a rip current. They have developed strong swimming skills, know the cause of this condition and can perform in demanding environments. When something unexpected happens, they have the knowledge, confidence and ability to jump right in.

Commanding- In this zone, you have taken control of your life. There are no lines around this zone because you decide the limits. Life happens on your terms and compromising no longer has to be an option. In this zone, you have established foundational habits and a thirst for knowledge. You refuse to relinquish your lead over the competition and take decisive action. You have developed the tools to cope with adversity and have high confidence in your abilities. When someone sees you operating in this zone, they will probably be envious or impressed. Chances are they don't have the freedom and earning potential you do. People who operate in this zone seem happier. Working hard is not arduous because they are working on their passion. People in this zone take risks, build companies and impact our everyday lives. They also create their own gravity and surround themselves with high achievers.

Visually, I would compare someone in the commanding zone to Diana Nyad's successful attempt to swim from Cuba to Florida. She completed this 52 hour 54 minute 18.6 second swim at the age of 64, without the aid of a shark cage. After four failed attempts, she developed the knowledge to handle challenges in the open ocean and skills to succeed in an evolving environment. When her record breaking day came, she had confidence in her planning, as well as resources and skills to overcome what many saw as an impossible challenge. She was in control and no one else's perceived limits could confine her.

"Isn't life about determining your own finish line?" - *Diana Nyad*

Anxious speaker

"Experience is the hardest kind of teacher. It gives you the test first and the lesson afterward." -Oscar Wilde

At one of my assignments, I had a person who shied away from the limelight. She didn't have a reputation as a self-starter and her reclusiveness impeded her chances for promotion. After some very direct feedback and self-examination on her part, she made a decision to do something radically new for herself; Public Speaking!

To some this may not seem like a leap, but for her it was terrifying. Two hurdles she faced upfront were; self-confidence engaging large groups and developing large red spots on her face and neck when she spoke. In spite of these challenges, she set a goal of five public speaking engagements over her next rating period. As a result, we assigned her to deliver training for large groups, lead team meetings and take on key responsibilities within our organization.

As time went on, she stayed committed to her goal. If I hadn't set something up for a while, she would gently remind me of my oversight and I'd find her a new opportunity. Of course, she stumbled along the way but as her supervisor, I continued to encourage her and keep her focused on the positive outcomes of her efforts. As she made positive changes in her life, her confidence grew and she became known for all the right reasons. It has been an amazing experience to watch her progress and transform from a timid, unengaged worker bee, to a person who confronts life head on and accepts the challenges along the way.

The definition of insanity is doing the same thing and expecting different results. This person finally realized that doing the same thing would keep her in the same place for the rest of her career. Therefore, she stepped out of her comfort zone and started a chain reaction that transformed her career, life and outlook!

Trust competent leaders (advice to subordinates)

"A leader is one who knows the way, goes the way and shows the way." -John C. Maxwell

For some of us, letting another person take care of our careers can be unsettling. If we aren't the ones taking measured actions, bugging our supervisors or pushing the envelope, we think we'll fall behind. In most cases, I would say this is a safe bet, since hardly anyone will take better care of your career than you. However, I have found one exception to this rule. When you find a competent leader who you trust and believe has your best interest in mind, let them take the reins.

I know this might sound a bit crazy but let me tell you why. When you finally meet a supervisor or leader that's capable of taking care of you, they will be deliberately putting things in place on your behalf. You will get comprehensive feedback to improve your weaknesses, opportunities that compliment your strengths and a clear perspective on operating within a team. If you keep taking independent actions, you will probably muddy the big picture this person is trying to paint for you. Now, this doesn't mean you should stop working hard or be less persistent. I'm just asking you to pause when you discover an opportunity and get their perspective before leaping in. When they recommend an opportunity you may not agree with, trust them and take it on with an open mind. When they move you from a position you're comfortable with, don't get irritated. Often times they are setting you up for positions or opportunities where you can excel. In my experience, great leaders will be transparent with their intent, so if you are ever confused and want to know their "Why", just ask!

On my teams, I tell members, *"If you take care of others, I'll take care of you! However, if you're always focused on taking care of yourself, you are doing my job so I guess I don't need to do it."* What I mean by this is, if everyone on a team is building others up, pitching in, sharing knowledge or taking the initiative to assist, the whole team gets better. If I have an efficiently running team, I have more time to develop those in my care. If I have more time to develop those in my care, I can set people up with opportunities and find areas to push growth.

In your work center, helping your co-workers and giving time back to supervisors will almost always benefit you. These actions will likely be recognized for their positive contributions and you will probably be rewarded with opportunities that enhance your career. People want to help people that help others. So do something different! Stop worrying about yourself and instead focus on making those around you better and giving your supervisor back time. If you do these two things, I am confident you will go farther than you would have going it alone.

For us spiritual people out there, I have learned to apply this principle in my relationship with God. Sometimes I try so hard to make my own path that I don't allow God's plan to develop in my life. Even when I see it coming together, I make selfish decisions because I think I know better than Him. Putting my life in His hands hasn't been easy but I have learned to leave my comfort zone, turn it all over to Him and allow God's plan to guide my path. As a result, I have been open to opportunities I would have not otherwise been available to take and am thankful for the transformational people He's put in my life along the way.

Let it go (advice to superiors)

"Someone who needs to control their environment is someone who's motivated by fear." -Tina Gilbertson

Believe it or not, some people have a hard time letting stuff go, especially when it comes to work related tasks. You probably know these folks as meddlers, control freaks or micromanagers; I just call them M&Ms. Most of the time, M&Ms don't even realize what they are doing because they have developed internal justifications to rationalize their intrusive behaviors. And just like an M&M, these people are always trying to control the chocolatey goodness of their team with their inflexible, hard candy shell.

Some of my favorite M&Ms sayings are, *"I just want to make sure the team has what it needs!"* Well, if you knew what the team needed to complete the task and wanted them to be successful, wouldn't you have supplied it up front?

How about, *"Can I give you some pointers?"* In my experience this means your efforts are lacking and you need to be revectored to the correct way of doing things.

I am convinced this group of people believes their inputs or involvement is so crucial to the success of a task, that they can't step back to let others take full ownership. But as I have learned, keeping things within arm's reach doesn't allow people to succeed or fail on their own terms. It doesn't allow someone to feel the full angst of realizing they were ill prepared or bear the weight of a presentation that falls flat. It does not allow someone to face a challenge and overcome it with an "Aha" moment. It doesn't allow someone to experience the full exhilaration of nailing an assignment and feeling the sense of accomplishment when words of affirmation come pouring in. By meddling, M&Ms steal small victories from the people they have entrusted to get the job done. As a result, they rob their people of career defining moments, take away from their story and diminish experiences that initiate growth.

If you're an M&M, step away from your comfort zone of control. Equip your folks with the skills and resources they need before assigning them a task, then LET IT GO! Who knows, you might learn something new, be taken back by their ingenuity or finally see their true potential.

Your subordinate has expectations for you. Ask what they are!

When you conduct a feedback session is it a lecture or a conversation?

I've had many initial feedback sessions that involved my supervisor telling me what to do, or his/her expectations but rarely have I been asked what I expected from my supervisor. Why is that? If a supervisor doesn't know your needs, how do they help you grow? If you don't convey what motivates you or the type of recognition you prefer, how can they effectively show their appreciation for a job well done?

At the end of every feedback session, I always ask my subordinates for their expectations of me or how I can best take care of them. The first time I ask this question I usually get a confused look. However, for those who don't know what they want yet, this simple question gets them thinking about their needs. Additionally, it helps them realize that every person wants to be cared for differently and the relationship between us is interactive, not static.

The old Golden rule of, *"Treat others the way you want to be treated"* is outdated. If you've not heard of the Platinum rule yet, it states, *"Treat others the way they want to be treated."* And since we all have different needs, motivations and goals, wouldn't you agree that this approach serves your people better?

Learn a different work language

"A different language is a different vision of life." - *Federico Fellini*

If you want to get new things accomplished in your work center, you may need to understand or speak different work languages. Large organizations tend to have several work languages within their departments, sections or divisions. When spoken outside of their tribes, these terms can have different meanings and cause confusion. If you are required to interface with sections outside of your own, my advice would be to sit down with those teams, attend some meetings and learn how to understand them better. This small effort will allow you to more effectively communicate your message in ways they understand.

As an example, the military has its own language with many different dialects. If you were to ask a Space Operator to explain their mission to a Fighter Pilot, you'd probably see a slight breakdown in communication. I believe this occurs because of the different worlds they live in. A Space Operator lives in a non-kinetic world, typically commutes home after their mission is complete, has longer timelines for decision making and the consequences of a mistake will almost never cost them their life.

On the other hand, a Fighter Pilot lives in a kinetic world, their mission requires them to operate in close proximity to an adversary, they spend significant amounts of time away from home, they must make split second life or death decisions and they face constant threats from every warfighting domain.

These differences shape their language, priorities and culture. As a result of living in these two distinctly unique environments, they communicate in very different ways and at times, these communication differences create impedance to integrated actions on the battlefield. To overcome these differences, people with experience in both kinetic and non-kinetic missions, such as Intelligence Analysts, are helpful translators between the two worlds.

In industry, language differences between an engineer and sales person can produce the same effect. One is centered on details or technical terms while the other is focused on big ideas with marketing in mind. When they speak, they tend to have difficulties relaying information. This is because one side wants to express how exciting a new technology is and the other is trying to figure out how a product or service serves their customers. This divergence can keep synergies from forming across the divisions and encumbers the exchange of information for an upcoming product or service. Consequently, the resulting communication to customers is suboptimal and key features or selling points may not be given the attention they deserve.

In some ways, I would compare the language differences within an organization to the romance languages of Portuguese and Spanish. When either is spoken, most people probably assume the communication is in Spanish. However, if you know them both, you will quickly realize which dialect is being used. Additionally, you will understand that the vernacular can be significantly different and that in order to get each side to understand the other, common terms or phases may need to be used. Here are a few words to demonstrate the differences between these two languages.

"Cena" in Portuguese translates to *"scene"* but in Spanish it means *"dinner."*

"Largo" in Portuguese translates to *"wide"* but in Spanish it means *"long."*

"Polvo" in Portuguese translates to *"octopus"* but in Spanish it means *"powder."*

As you can see, if someone started speaking Portuguese to a Spanish speaker, there might be occasions where thoughts are lost in translation. Trying to communicate without knowing the links and differences between the two languages can lead to confusion. Confusion can cause important information to be lost, rendering the communication ineffective. As a result, uncertain actions might occur and people on either side of a conversation may understand the desired outcome differently.

So leave your work language comfort zone and find ways to integrate with people in other missions or departments. Step out and become the translator for your organization. Not only will this help your organizational efforts, but chances are this move will look good on you too.

Get Moving!

Now that you know how to get out of your comfort zone and where to go when you leave, Get Moving! Staying where you are isn't getting you where you want to go. Try something uncomfortable and trust a leader to push you beyond your limits. Let your people take calculated risks and give up control, even if it scares you. Learn another work language and be the translator that brings the tribes together. But most of all, never settle for staying in your comfort zone. It's not serving you well!

Question 1: What zone are you in?

Question 2: What zone do you want to be in?

Question 3: What can you let go at work?

Question 4: How do M&Ms effect your motivation?

Question 5: What expectations do you have for your supervisor?

Question 6: What work language do you need to learn? How would it improve your operations?

HOW RESISTANCE LEADS TO RESILIENCE

"By three methods we may learn wisdom: First by reflection which is the noblest; Second, by imitation, which is the easiest; and third by experience which is the bitterest."
-Confucius

Have you ever worked in an organization that felt full of resistance? Maybe you noticed it shortly after joining and its presence could be sensed in meetings, projects or relationships. It almost feels like an aura of *"No"* just hangs in the air. Maybe it came on gradually as new initiatives or management directed changes were implemented, or you started noticing it as you sought advancement in your career. So, what creates this atmosphere? In some organizations I have seen resistance originate from the person in charge. In others it seems to be a part of their culture. However, in almost every case there appears to be a one or two key people driving this ambiance. For them, something new or risky is uncomfortable and potentially damaging to their reputation. I don't believe they want to say *"No"* but must have a clear reason to say *"Yes."* So how do you operate in these environments? Read on!

Being yourself when people resist you

"Be yourself; everyone else is already taken." -Oscar Wilde

For starters, sometimes in life you will find yourself surrounded by people who just don't get you. They don't understand who or what you are, so they try to change you. They do this by finding a person they like and encourage you to follow their example. When you find yourself in this position, maintain your identity because being someone else is not sustainable.

At one of my organizations, I felt like the leadership team wanted me to be someone else. It seemed as if everything I did encountered resistance. My big personality, extrovert behaviors, witty comments and curious mind just didn't seem to fit in. Even when asking for simple feedback, their responses would be something vague or superficial like, *"Well you said this one comment about our partner relationship six months ago and I don't think that was an accurate description."* SIX MONTHS AGO? If you didn't like my comment, why did you stew on it so long? As time went on, I came to the conclusion that being myself was detrimental to my career.

Since it was clear to me that I wasn't going to get the type of feedback I needed to grow, I searched for insight. I began by paying attention to the behaviors of my peers and focused on traits our leadership team applauded. As I observed their interactions, I discovered that our leadership team did not respond well to divergent ideas or actions. They wanted a methodical approach for every act and sought to avoid any real risk. Additionally, they wanted a "Yes Man" who would not respectfully challenge their ideas and would complete every task in the manner they wanted it done.

Basically, you were empowered to do things the way they wanted them done, not the way you wanted to do them. Furthermore, at times the way you completed a task seemed just as important as the task itself.

After deciphering which behaviors they liked best, I decided for the sake of my career, I would try to fit their mold. Specifically, this meant attempting to emulate a person who embodied the actions they valued most. To do so, I had to suppress almost every quality that made me, *"me."* In the weeks and months ahead, I felt as if I lost my identity and I slowly slipped into depression. On one side, I started receiving praise for my so called "maturation" but on the other, I felt like an impostor. The things that made me unique faded away and the grey suited world of Joe vs. the Volcano became my everyday life. I literally felt like I was dying inside but did my best to hide this decay from the outside world.

After some time, walking through the front door began feeling like entering the gates of hell. One day I finally broke down and on my way to work, took a detour to the emergency room for intense suicidal thoughts. That was my tipping point and I knew things would have to change if I wanted to survive. As I sought help through the mental health system, I realized that keeping my identity was paramount to my sanity. I also decided to be myself at all costs because being someone else almost cost me everything.

In the weeks after, I started being my genuine self again. I also began acknowledging my rough edges and underwent an effort to round them down. I began paying attention to how my actions were being received and worked on better methods to achieve my desired outcomes. I sought to understand the perspectives of others and found authentic approaches to engage in group activities. Although I did not receive many compliments for this so called "regression" I was much happier and could look myself in the mirror without disgust. Throughout all this I came to realize that, *"WHAT MAKES US DIFFERENT, MAKES A DIFFERENCE"* and every person's perspective and contribution has value, including mine.

What I work towards now is becoming a better version of myself. I keep my essence but also acknowledge there is always room for improvement. I have accepted that sometimes you aren't a good fit for a leadership team or another person's personality; and that's ok. Even when you can't see eye to eye, I have learned to understand the importance of their views and explore their reasoning to make better decisions. Additionally, when a relationship breaks down I always seek to maintain a foundation of respect. You can withstand the ebbs and flows of conflict if respect is present but if someone feels disrespected, it can inflict lasting damage.

Haters are gonna hate! Thank you for the inspiration!

On 15 May 2020, I got my first 1 star review on Amazon. No comments, no name. Just a click and send without feedback or a conversation. Could this person have been a vague character in the book that I shared a negative experience with? Maybe! Could it have been a person I upset at some point in my career? Possibly! Or could it be someone who just didn't like the writing? I have no clue and at this stage in my life, I'm ok with not knowing. Why? Because I have learned that no matter what you do in life, you will always have critics. Additionally the more you seek to achieve, the more critics you will have. Here are some other personal truths I have discovered about negative actions or critics.

1.   Negative actions connect us just as much as positive ones. Most people understand how a positive action creates connection but just think of how strong the connection is between a thief or murder and the family they impacted. Their stories are intertwined and the only way to break that bond is by forgiving and letting that person go. If you feel the need to exact revenge, guess what? You are choosing to stay connected and allowing someone else's negative action keep you from pursing more fruitful things in life.

2.   If you are going to pursue your passion, accept haters. Some people won't see your vision and will criticize your actions; and that's ok. They don't see the world like you do and they have no skin in the game, so press on with your dream and believe in yourself. Trust me; you will spend way more time building your dream than they will tearing down.

3.   The right track has bumps. Almost every time I have been on the right track in life, I have encountered bumps. For me, this is spiritual warfare and I believe it's the dark side trying to keep me from making a positive difference in this world. When I pursue things of no consequence, I rarely face challenges. Therefore, I've come to learn that when I'm seeking to do something significant, bumps in the road are my confirmation I'm headed in the right direction.

In conclusion, I want to say thank you to the person who left that review. You have confirmed that I am on the right path. I am responding in this fashion because I want to stay connected to you. You are now a part of my story and I hope our connection brings positive change to your life.

Everyday resistance: Colorado life compared to Difficult Organizations

"It is not the strongest or most intelligent who will survive but those who can best manage change." -Charles Darwin

Midway through my military career, I moved from Maryland to Colorado. As I transitioned between these dissimilar landscapes, I came to discover how unseen forces affected me. In this section, I'll explain these forces, link them to situations in difficult organizations and provide advice on how to overcome them. Additionally, I'll step you through everyday living, running and climbing in Colorado and compare it to the challenges you might face in a difficult organization. Like living in Colorado, difficult organizations have underlying resistances you must contend with every day.

Everyday living

Upon arriving in Colorado, you might notice that little things such as walking are a slightly more difficult. This persistent resistance is called altitude and once you experience it, you'll recognize its presence. As you adjust to the effects of altitude, the best course of action is to be patient and immerse yourself in the atmosphere before participating in strenuous activities. Once acclimated, you will establish a new physical baseline and better understand how this force affects you.

The same principle applies in the workplace. Take time to understand the culture you are entering into. Chances are it's a little different than you're used to. Observe the personal interactions, determine what leadership values and adjust your daily activities to assimilate.

Colorado is also home to extremely dry air. This may not seem daunting but it's an element that's more impactful than you think. Your lungs like humidity. That's why we put on humidifiers when we're sick or enjoy taking in a deep misty breath by a waterfall. Our sinuses, throats and lungs want a bit of moisture to keep things feeling right. However, the climate of Colorado is dry and requires you to supplement for its lack of moisture. The first step to counter this arid climate is to drink lots of water. Since your body isn't getting the moisture it wants from the environment, you must deliberately increase your fluid intake to offset this deficiency. If you choose not to, you can become dehydrated, develop dry skin or find yourself with a headache or bloody nose.

In a difficult organization, the dry climate you may face is pessimism. Pessimism can suck the life out of you and the people around you. If you find yourself in this type of environment, find a group of people who focus on the positives. If they don't exist, you might have to create your own optimism by reading or listening to positive messages. Like drinking water, you must be deliberate and consistent in the consumption of positive information if you want to remain hydrated in pessimistic work environments.

Running

If you choose to start running in Colorado, you should always account for the everyday resistances like altitude and dry air. These influences have become your new baseline and will be evident for every action you take.

Once you get acclimated to the general climate of Colorado, you may decide to start running. In a difficult organization, this translates to getting significant things accomplished. If you go for a run in Colorado, start by being prepared. This means accepting the effects of altitude on your run and remaining hydrated every day.

For your work center, this goes back to understanding your workplace culture and creating an atmosphere of optimism. Maintaining a positive mind set is especially important during this step since it's the only aspect you can control. If you're going to take on something difficult, you might as well bring a full tank of good attitude with you.

Second, to make running more enjoyable you should consider when the best time is to go. In Colorado, windy conditions build throughout the day and by afternoon the wind and weather can be extreme. These developments tend to make running later in the day less pleasant; but it can be avoided. Go running early! Colorado mornings are typically cool and calm. By going early, you can meet your objective before the extreme afternoon conditions have a chance to build. Of course, you can still go for a run later in the day but you will increase your chances of encountering wind, rain and sometimes hail. That's because you chose to give the resistant energies ample time to build before taking action.

This same principle can be applied in your professional life! If you move on your tasks or goals early, you can get things done before resistance builds against you. If you wait to take action, the resistant energies at work have time to grow. This delay makes room for competing ideas, arguments and entrenched thinking. Once these forces build, you will likely face more pushback. Instead, don't allow the critics, time wasters and nay-sayers to develop a case against you. Move out early while their thoughts are still formulating and their resistance is weak.

Climbing

If you are really feeling up to the challenge, in Colorado or at work, at some point you will want to climb a mountain. Be aware though, the forces that made things challenging at the lower effort tiers will be even more present at this level. The increased effects of altitude will make each step up more laborious, proper hydration is even more important and weather during the ascent can be more extreme.

Besides the other elements we've already discussed, one new obstacle you might encounter when climbing the mountain is snow. This ground cover can slow your pace and obscure the most direct route to the summit.

In the workplace, snow can mimic navigating relationships that prolong your journey or personalities that complicate your ascent.

If you make it through the snow, you will eventually end up at the tree line. Once you cross this point, your goal will be in sight but you will also be exposed to the most extreme weather on the mountain. No more tree protection, no hiding places; it's just you against the elements.

In a work center, the tree line represents the senior management corps. These people can give you a clear view of the summit or create forces that make the last leg of your journey harder. Chances are, many of them rose to their position by adhering to the status quo. For toeing the company line, they have probably been rewarded with promotions and may be wary of strangers in their environment. If you want to reach the top, you will need to grind through this unprotected landscape and prepare yourself to face the extremes of every resistance you've encountered along the way.

The Takeaway

If you hone your skills in resistance filled environments, you give yourself an advantage when your circumstances improve. For the same reason Olympians and endurance athlete's exercise at high altitudes, developing your skills in arduous environments enhances the effects training. This gives them an advantage when competing in low altitude, humid locations such as Florida. So use the opposing forces of your current environment to increase your resilience. If you develop these skills where it's challenging, you're more likely to succeed in organizations or situations where the climate is benign.

When you get shot down, change your trajectory

"Come to accept that if your methods don't change, neither will your results." -Steve Maraboll

Have you ever had a boss who seemed to shoot down every idea you presented? No matter what you tried, your balloon was popped and your energy diminished. Well maybe your ideas aren't the problem; maybe it's your delivery!

I had this issue at one of my work centers and for the longest time, I could not figure out what was wrong. Everywhere else I had been, I felt like I was able to communicate my ideas with ease, but not there! After a while I began to doubt myself and shrank every time my name was called. I could not figure out the hiccup, until one day when we all received the results of a personality test. It was a "Eureka" moment! On the screen that day, I saw the personality preferences of my leadership team and I, and truth be told we could not have been more different. All four of them came in as ISTJ's (Introverted, Sensing, Thinking,

Judging) and I stood alone as an ENTP (Extroverted, Intuition, Thinking, Perceiving). An almost completely opposite personality type!

To be specific, in this situation the personality based communication barrier I kept encountering resulted from the differences in our second letters, S and N. This personality trait focuses on how people prefer to take in information.

A Sensing (S) person focuses on the reality of how things are. They pay attention to facts and details and like things described in specific, literal ways. This was my leadership team.

Conversely, Intuition (N) people like me, enjoy imagining all of the possibilities. They like big picture ideas, seeing how things connect and prefer descriptions using figurative and poetic methods.

This epiphany helped me finally realize why my attempts at communication kept failing. I was delivering information in a way our top four leaders did not prefer. As I researched their personality type, I learned their preferences for accepting information and adapted my methods to be more effective. With this new information in hand, I was finally able to adjust my aim and hit the communication target.

As I investigated this scenario further, I discovered that the underlying issue in this scenario was my preference to deliver messages with the big picture in mind. I tried using concepts and emotions to persuade them, when they wanted logic and details to be convinced. They needed to understand the in's and out's of my proposed ideas. They wanted to know when, where, how and any other detail I could provide. Their preference to receive this information was using a highly detailed presentation, preferably accompanied with visual charts and statistics.

On the contrary, my approach rarely used a computer. I thought slides and details were distracting and sought to paint a picture using enthusiastic words and positive energy. In retrospect, I'm guessing my delivery method resembled that of a starry eyed teen more than it did a well thought out, purposeful endeavor.

Repeating my mistake without considering the root cause resulted in a consistent state of failed communication. What I should have been targeting was their receiving preference and devising a delivery method that increased my odds of hitting the target.

If you are experiencing this issue in your work center, take some time to look at personality type indicators like Myers-Briggs and see if you can figure out the personality type of the person you're trying to reach. As you learn about their preferences, you will discover specific ways to communicate with them. With this knowledge, you can then develop a new approach and increase your chances of making a successful connection.

Be a donkey in the hole

"You may see me struggle but you will never see me quit" -Tom Coleman

This story is an old tale but I think its relevant today. Enjoy.

One day a farmer's donkey fell down into a well. The animal cried pitifully for hours as the farmer weighted his options. Finally, he determined the animal was not worth saving and the well was a hazard that needed covering up;

so he decided to bury the donkey.

Soon after, the farmer invited his neighbors over to help. They all grabbed shovels and began throwing dirt into the well. When the donkey realized what was happening, he cried horribly. Then to everyone's amazement he quieted down. A few shovel loads later, the farmer was astonished by what he saw.

With each shovel of dirt that hit the donkey's back, he'd shake it off and step up. As the farmer's neighbors continued to shovel dirt on top of the animal, he'd shake it off and step up. Pretty soon, everyone watched in amazement as the donkey stepped out of the well and trotted off!

The moral is that sometimes you may find yourself in a position where you feel like you are being buried alive. When you are at this low point, every negative moment feels like life is piling on. Like the farmer, our friends may ponder solutions for our predicaments but ultimately it is on us to save ourselves. Refuse to let life bury you! Shake off every heap of dirt or negative experience and stand taller on the wisdom you gain. If you keep at it, never give up and learn how to get out of life's low points, you will find yourself trotting away from adversity like a donkey that was in a hole.

Quotes to change your mindset about failures

"I never lose. I either win or I learn!" -Nelson Mandela

"You may encounter many defeats, but you must not be defeated. In fact, it may be necessary to encounter the defeats, so you can know who you are, what you can rise from, how you can still come out of it." -Maya Angelou

"I have not failed. I have just found 10,000 ways that won't work." -Thomas A. Edison

"Success is not final, failure is not fatal: it is the courage to continue that counts." -Winston S. Churchill

"A thinker sees his own actions as experiments and questions--as attempts to find out something. Success and failure are for him answers above all." -Friedrich Nietzsche

"Failure is simply the opportunity to begin again, this time more intelligently." -Henry Ford

"Failure is instructive. The person who really thinks learns quite as much from his failures as from his successes." -John Dewey

Grow a deep taproot

"Deep roots are not reached by the frost." -J.R.R. Tolkien

Plants provide a great example of using resistance to gain resilience. Plants are made up of two types of root systems; taproot and fibrous.

A taproot plant grows deep into the ground. Think about a dandelion. If you have ever tried to pull a dandelion out of the ground, you know how difficult it can be. Most of the time you only get the top out and the roots hold strong, ready to sprout forth again. Dandelions are resilient and once established are extremely hard to eradicate. They survive when droughts come because they are dug in and have evolved to resist numerous challenges.

On the other hand, fibrous root plants have roots that

grow out closer to the surface. Think about corn. Corn can grow nice and tall but is easily pulled from the ground. If a strong storm hits, corn can blow over causing fatal damage.

So have a deep tap root. Keep digging until you find what you need. Go deep when the rain stops. Stay rooted when the droughts come and the winds blow. Stay hardy! Persevere! Resist! And in the end when adversity ceases, be ready to sprout forth again.

Let resistance be the force that strengthens you

"You never really know how strong you are until being strong is the only choice you have." -Unknown

Resistance is necessary if you want to become stronger. Just as a muscle needs weight resistance to change, you need life resistance to change as well. Let resistance be the force that transforms you into a better leader. Let resistance make you a better person. Put negative moments beneath you and build a solid foundation from those experiences. Resistance is an opportunity for growth, if you embrace it! Learn from resistance, accept wisdom as its reward and apply the knowledge to positively impact your life and the lives of others.

Question 1: How can you develop into a better version of yourself?

Question 2: What are the resistant forces in your organization?

Question 3: What steps can you take to perform through this resistance?

Question 4: How should you change your message

delivery to hit your target?

Question 5: What have you learned from your failures?

PROMOTE COLLEGIALITY OVER COMPETITION

"Competition has been shown to be useful up to a certain point and no further, but cooperation, which is the thing we must strive for today, begins where competition leaves off." - Franklin D. Roosevelt

Have you ever worked in an environment that pitted worker against worker, section against section and so on? You're part of so called "team" yet the reward system favors individual achievements, prompting people to focus on tasks that primarily benefit themselves. Eventually, people's actions become focused on standing out amongst their peers. Why? So they can enjoy short term personal recognition over long term team success!

I believe our society favors individual achievement over team success. You can see this in sports when a game is won by a whole team effort, yet someone in the media feels the need to declare an MVP. In some games the team contribution is so significant that you aren't even sure who they'll name. Nonetheless, they chose some individual who usually gives the credit right back to the team.

It's like we can't help ourselves. Our culture needs a hero and we obviously like judging people for their herculean efforts. As a result of our cultural bias, the media develops captivating tales of heroism and bombards us with the story. However, I think this mindset is flawed and individual achievements are built for a sprint, not a marathon.

Collegiality (col·le·gi·al·i·ty)

Are you familiar with this word? Do you know what it means? How to pronounce it? Most people I run across don't and for a valid reason; because our society fixates on competition over collegiality. You see competition in sports, politics, television shows, work centers, etc... and it's always depicted as two competing sides, ideas or principles. However, if we created more cooperative relationships in our lives, I believe we'd build more words like this into our vocabulary.

Merriam-Webster dictionary defines "Collegiality" as the cooperative relationship of colleagues. When you look at other sources, you see terms and phrases like companionship, shared responsibility and working together to do a job.

When I think of the challenges we face in our modern work centers or about the hyper competitive world outside of our organizations, wouldn't you agree that internal collegiality over competition is what we should really be aiming for?

A Chicken story

"Not everything that can be counted counts, and not everything that counts can be counted." -Albert Einstein

In the 1990's, William M. Muir, Professor of Animal Sciences at Purdue University, conducted an experiment meant to increase the egg-laying productivity of hens. The study was comprised of two groups, each containing nine chickens. The first group consisted of the most productive "Superstar" chickens and the second was made up of an average group of hens. These groups were left alone to breed for six generations and at the end of this period, Dr. Muir measured their productivity to see which group performed best.

Before reading on, guess which group had the highest productivity at the end of the study?

The study concluded that the average group of hens was happier, healthier and actually producing more eggs than they were at the beginning of the experiment. In fact, their egg production increased by 160% over this period. They had harmony and an environment that allowed them to sustainably grow as a team.

In a work center, this would resemble a team built with diversity, having different strengths, weaknesses, perspectives, experiences and backgrounds. Overall, diversity creates less team deficiencies and provides opportunities to build on similar past competencies. It's like the secret sauce for a well-rounded team.

On the other hand, after aggressively pecking each other to death, the "Superstar" group only had three chickens left. It seems with all the competition in their work center, the high performers started suppressing their peers instead of living up to their potential. As a result, their egg productivity plummeted and the ones that survived looked like they'd been put through hell.

The results of this experiment can easily be applied to our work centers. To me, this experiment demonstrates how measuring an individual's output might not be a good overall indicator of their worth to a team. Just because one is great, doesn't make a bunch of them together, better! In some high visibility projects, several high performers may find themselves thrown together into a team. At times this collaboration works, but when it doesn't produce the expected outcome, people always wonder why. In most cases, I think it comes down to egos and a refusal to focus on team unity as a goal.

I've felt this way several times throughout my military career. For my story, I always felt like I had to decide between integrating into a team and standing out amongst the masses. At the lower ranks, I wanted to believe both were possible but I never seemed to find the balance. It was either, *"Stand up and be recognized"* or *"Who are you?"* When I choose to join the team, I felt like my career advancement was put on hold. Consequently, when I pursued personal career advancement I felt like others labeled me as selfish. After I stopped worrying about promotions, I thought back and imagined how impactful I might have been if I had selflessly contributed to every one of my teams over the course of my career. Had I believed that teamwork was more highly regarded than personal achievement, I know my behavior would have evolved to align with that purpose. However, because I saw leadership teams valuing individual effort, I consistently sought to stand out from the crowd.

A Sports Analogy

"Talent wins games, but teamwork and intelligence win championships."-Michael Jordan

The New England Patriots, whether you like them or not, have been one of the most successful, consistent sports teams over the last two decades. They have one superstar, several key players, committed role players and a regular rotation of very talented athletes. Their management team knows how everyone plugs in, their strengths and weaknesses, how to handle unexpected absences and provide a clear vision on achieving a common goal. Even when their superstar or key players are out of a game, they still find a way to win because they have built their organization with the right mix of people for long term success. In their organization, everyone does their job, minimizes internal conflict and focuses on competing outside of their organization. This consistent and intentional effort has led to nine Super Bowl appearances in the last twenty years and six World Champion titles.

On the other hand, the 2011 Philadelphia Eagles were supposed to be the "Dream Team" of the football world and were given 15-2 odds to win the Super Bowl that year. They had tons of big name players and all the talent they could want. So why did they finish at 8-8 and fail to qualify for the playoffs? I believe the main reason was because each Superstar competed to lead the newly formed team and they never learned how to coexist for the betterment of the organization.

This story is not some anomaly either. In sports and business, you can read story after story about big names being thrown together in a team only to find their anticipated results falling short of expectations. In some cases, I believe the underlying issues could have been overcome by valuing team above all and promoting collective goals over individual prowess. I also believe setting a tone of collegiality over competition will guide your team, division or organization to consistent outcomes and recurrent success. If I had to choose, I would rather be seen as a steady light in the night sky as opposed to a firework that sparkles and inevitably fades away.

Working in a toxic environment

"When a workplace becomes toxic, its poison spreads beyond its walls and into the lives of its workers and their families." -Gary Chapman

I know first-hand about working in a toxic work environment fueled by excessive competition and relentless peer suppression. At the beginning of this story, everything in the organization seemed great. We had a new group of people, everyone was excited to build something from the ground up and the mood was optimistic. Although there was a little talk of competition, it did not seem like it would control our lives for the next two years. After a few months though, this all changed and the culture became one of relentless competition.

In this unit, competition manifested itself in many ways. Some of the obvious ways included additional rewards for exceptionally high physical fitness test scores, internal stratification boards and a slide by slide comparison of each sections administrative metrics.

In regards to physical fitness tests, each week a slide was presented with the latest scores and names next to them. The only time a name was absent from the scoreboard was when someone had failed their test, but in a unit of forty people it was obvious whose names were omitted. The highest scores were praised and anything less would receive some belittling comments from the group. Even if you achieved the best score of your career, finally met a personal goal or had a ten percent improvement, your individual accomplishment was not considered valuable. The only thing that mattered was how you measured up against others! After a while, you could see that people weren't even proud of their fitness achievements anymore. They knew they couldn't compete with the score of a twenty year old single person or an over forty on the verge of any empty nest, so they just stopped trying. Once, I earned a 97.6% while managing a family with two young children, working daily in a toxic environment and battling though mental health struggles. I was proud of this score and worked hard to get it but since I didn't have the highest score on the spreadsheet, the clucking hens chimed in and reminded me that I still didn't measure up.

Competition was also evident in our weekly staff meetings. Each week the four section leads were required to put our administrative metrics on a slide to be presented in front of our leadership team. The best would be rewarded with verbal affirmation and everyone else was required to defend their numbers. Nothing about the actual mission or individual workload was taken into account. Looking good administratively became the top priority! In my opinion, this was because our next tier leadership heavily evaluated these items and our Commander could not handle being bested by other associated units. After a while, our Commanders desire to have her unit be represented as the best in the Group wore us out and pitted us against each other. If your numbers didn't make the cut, the questions from leadership increased and your individual effort levels had to go up. If your numbers came up on top, other section leads would throw you under the bus, minimize your achievements or attempt to one up the person receiving admiration.

After a while, unconstructive comments became common place, such as, *"If I did nothing else all day, my numbers would be that good too!"*

"Sorry, I was busy taking care of your people because they didn't feel comfortable coming to you."

"Is the mission or admin more important?" And the list

goes on and on!

It got to the point where no one left a staff meeting without a bruise. In turn, we all grew more frustrated and defensive with each other. Personally, I can't think of a single time where I felt compelled to help a colleague after going through one of those slug fests.

In another case, the leadership team decided to internally stratify our NCOs (Non-Commissioned Officers) and SNCOs (Senior Non-Commissioned Officers) to see who they should promote. I remember one stratification board in particular, when we had three people eligible to promote to Master Sergeant. In front of us was the career records of all three members and we were prompted to debate on who was ready for a promotion. After all the talking was done, we held a vote for each person and all three received the majority needed to get promoted, but that's not what happened. Instead, only the person with the best metrics was promoted. Her lack of people skills and leadership experience was in no way considered in this decision. Among the other two, one had great interpersonal skills and people from all sections came to him to for advice. The other person was incredibly knowledgeable and a team player that willingly helped anyone. In my opinion, all three had their strengths and weaknesses and they should have all been promoted. The two that weren't, were told that they needed to be evaluated more before a promotion could be approved. To me, this just meant we'll look at you again when your numbers get up.

Months went by without talk of promotion, resulting in daily frustrations and career uncertainty for the remaining two. Eventually, they discovered that metrics mattered most in our unit and their actions began to change. Instead of exhibiting their intrinsic teamwork focused behaviors, they sought to safeguard their careers and elevate their positions. That's when each section lead became an isolated island and the collaboration amongst us faded away.

In the months and years ahead our behaviors became protective, defensive, passive aggressive and at times directly aggressive. We spent so much time trying to cover our own butts that we wouldn't extend a helping hand when our peer was drowning. We'd smile when others messed up because we knew it created an opening. Additionally, since metrics were what mattered, our numbers became astonishingly good. In fact, it was a bit embarrassing for our external competition because our numbers were ten to twenty percent better than everyone else's. This caused a whole different set of issues because other organizations assumed we were trying to embarrass them and began to see us as an enemy as well.

Internally, we had no morale, no team and no sense of loyalty. We all hated going to work, three of us sought help for suicidal thoughts, I developed an auto immune disease that caused me to go bald and the entire experience is almost void of any pleasant memories. In fact, despite winning tons of awards there, the only positive memory I can recall is one of a sincere "Thank you." It was the only compliment I can remember feeling genuine.

As a final example, I discovered that even competing was a competition. I consider myself to be competitive person, so when put into a hyper competitive environment my spirited behaviors intensify. During my two and a half years there, I was SNCO of the Quarter six of ten times, SNCO of the Year for the Squadron and SNCO of the Year for the Group, number one of one hundred and thirty SNCOs! But did any of this matter? No! It was a complete waste of time and energy. I became a silo of excellence on an isolated prairie.

Although I did everything I thought I was supposed to, I still had to compete against my Commanders ideal version of a leader. Even with all of those accolades, she still refused to stratify me on an annual evaluation, despite the fact that there were only two eligible people in the entire Group. She also tried to influence my Supervisor to mark down my evaluation and talked poorly about me behind my back. I could not win and I could not compete against her ideas, so I spiraled into poor health and manufactured a perpetually distressed state of mind.

Admittedly, I was just as guilty as everyone else in constructing this toxic work center but at the time I believed these actions and behaviors were the only way to get ahead. In hindsight, what we should have been working towards, especially in a new unit, was developing a culture of collaboration, building each other up and creating an environment that drew people in. Instead, we all became feather plucked chickens and we never reached our true potential.

Doing something for a person you're in direct competition with?

"Doing nothing for others is the undoing of ourselves." - Horace Mann

One of my favorite senior leader interview questions is, *"What have you done to advance someone you're in direct competition with?"* I almost always get a look of confusion, then their mind starts racing and finally they answer with something like, *"Uhh, I helped this one guy move."*

The thought of affording an opportunity to someone you are competing with is ludacris, right? Well, I think it's the true mark of an unselfish, team oriented leader.

Of all the times I have asked this question, I have only ever had one response that seemed worthwhile. During an interview for a key leadership position, one applicant went out of his way to help another applicant apply for the same job. The first applicant was the interim team leader and was helping the other applicant because he was deployed and not in the loop for timelines. Some might have used this to their advantage and let the deployed guy fail, but not this person. Furthermore, the deployed guy was highly competitive and for many on the interview panel was the front runner. The applicant at home station knew this and still went out of his way to ensure the deployed member's application was complete and submitted on time anyway.

To shed a little more light on this scenario, the guy at home was not on the best footing when he applied for the position. He had just gone through some personal struggles and was recently passed over for other promotion opportunities, so he felt a bit vulnerable. Yet, knowing all this and having a history of things not going his way, he performed like a true professional and personally ensured his competition was able to apply on time for the position. It was one of the most selfless acts I have ever seen in my military career and it showed how much he cared for those on his team, even those he was competing against. He knowingly risked a rare promotion opportunity by being a genuine leader. For me, this was all I needed to give him my vote. He had the aptitude, drive and experience but above all, his unselfish actions to care for his competition showed me that he's the kind of leader that puts others first; and that's the kind of guy I want on my team.

For my story, there was a high visibility opportunity coming to our unit and since I was the highest performing person at the time, they offered it to me first. This opportunity would have come with a valuable formal education, meetings with industry leaders and desirable travel. Although this opportunity would have been great for me, I knew someone in my unit who had an interest in this field and would be intrinsically motivated to do a great job. As a result, I thanked them for their consideration and recommended the other person for the opportunity. I did this because I knew it was best for the unit, even if it wasn't best for me. He ultimately got the job and our mission was better for it.

Play beautiful music

"Alone we can do so little; together we can do so much." -Helen Keller

Do you think a hit song can be composed from one note? Of course not! You need variety to make it a success. The same principle applies to a team. Think about the difference between a single note tone, the twinge of several uncoordinated keys being played at once or the harmonious sound of a trained pianist striking a chord. It's a noticeable difference. That's because dissimilar things can either reveal their differences when poorly organized or can morph into something amazing when synchronized.

On a team of one, individual effort can seem like a pianist playing a single note. No matter how hard they try or how great the note being played is, eventually people will tire of it. As a result, the single note song will fade away and inevitably be forgotten.

A disjointed or competitive team resembles the noise of several unevaluated keys being played clumsily. When you hear it, each note will seem to step on the others and even the loudest tone gets lost in the chaos. On a team full of contention and competition, each member is trying to get their one note heard above all else. The resulting sound causes a visceral reaction to its listeners and any message attempting to be conveyed will be lost in the appalling consummation.

However, a well-run team with a skilled orchestrator can create lasting results. A trained pianist can put together harmonious keys, choose single notes that are strong on their own and unite it all into one pleasing song. As they identify and assemble notes and chords, the pianist can organize each individual segment to create a masterpiece.

On a team, a good leader sees how different people complement each other and combine their talents to create a hit. They will also be adept to know where individuals can insert their single notes and where the full bodied chords of a well-rounded team can give true essence to a song. When every part of the team is understood and employed in the correct fashion, your team can craft a melody that will sound like a symphony of success.

Where does competition belong?

Competition is not all bad and it definitely has its place in the work center but where should it belong most of the time?

Inside yourself and outside of your organization!

Internally, we should be competing with the person we know we can be. Michael Jordan did not compete against other people; every day he competed against the person he knew he could be and he became the greatest basketball player of all time. If he was competing against another player, he would not have pushed himself to greatness. If your organization is the best, don't try to compete against some lower skilled opponent. Compete against what you can be and continue to stay ahead of the pack.

Externally, we should compete against an opponent that produces a unifying emotion, not another team within your own organization. Chevy pushes themselves because of Ford, Google because of Microsoft and Airbus because of Boeing. In these situations, very clear goals can be set against their competition and leaders can rally their work force to prevail. It works because it's an Us vs. Them mentality and the entire team can unite behind a collective mindset to win. Structure your competition to focus on an external opponent and your internal achievements will rise.

Question 1: What does Collegiality look like in your work place?

Question 2: How have you assembled your flock of hens?

Question 3: How do you reward the people that make your team function effectively?

Question 4: Where does excessive internal competition exist in your organization?

Question 5: What are you doing to set the right culture for long term success?

Question 6: What goals are you trying to achieve and what kind of rewards are best to realize them?

SEE SOMETHING
DIFFERENT TO BE
SOMETHING DIFFERENT

"You and I possess within ourselves – at every moment of our lives, under all circumstances, the power to transform the quality of our lives. Knowing that is what the work is all about." -Werner Erhard

Transforming yourself takes effort and change is hard if you don't modify what you know. For this reason, you need to leave your little corner of the world and experience something different. College can be a good start but if you stay in the United States, it may not offer the diversity of experience you need to truly see life through a different lens. Travel abroad can be insightful as well, but if you stay at a resort you may miss the life changing encounters around you. If you really want to grow into something different, I suggest joining the military, going on a missionary trip or volunteering in a third world country. If you don't have access to these opportunities, the next best option might be to get involved in downtrodden areas of your community. These divergent environments are great places for seeing vantage points you probably know very little about.

How joining the Air Force changed my life

"Never write about a place until you're away from it, because that gives you perspective." -Ernest Hemingway

To begin, I am not bagging on my childhood. I grew up in a loving home and was surrounded by good people. I had two hard working parents who did their best to provide for my brother and I. Their lessons of hard work and doing things the right way will always stick with me, but there were certain personal needs they could not satisfy. For example, there was no one in my life who had attained the level of success I sought to achieve. I had no mentors for life's hard questions or to provide seasoned wisdom and deep insight. And I never met a person who'd seen enough of the world, to change my limited view of it.

To give you more perspective, my ultimate childhood goal was to own a $100,000 home. That achievement alone would have been my apex and anything above it would have been gravy! I believed my path to get there was to secure a job with a decent wage and minimum amount of training. With my limited view, I thought this poorly constructed plan would keep me from getting stuck in terrible jobs for the rest of my life. That was it! That was as far as my vision and surroundings took me. That was the bullseye I was aiming for, a $100,000 and decent job. This was what I wanted to reach at the end of my life and achieving these goals would have put me in a better position than most of the people I knew.

Looking back, I now realize how my lack of vision was keeping me from real success. When your ambitions are small, so are your actions. It wasn't until I left my environment, met drastically different people, had real life experiences and gained transformational knowledge that I started to see what I could become. More than anything else, that is the opportunity the Air Force gave me.

Joining the Air Force allowed me to leave my old life behind and see the world from a whole new angle. I was forced to grow up and take responsibility for my actions. For the first time, I was surrounded by people living a life I could have only imagined as a kid. The military is filled with highly motivated, incredibly intelligent and overtly ambitious people whose energy will infect you. At nearly every assignment, I have met a person or people that have changed my life for the better. I have had the privilege to travel the world, live in Europe and Asia, learn about other cultures and finally see lifestyles that align with my personal vision.

For me, a quote by Mark Twain sums up how I feel about the opportunities afforded to me throughout my Air Force experience.

"Travel is fatal to prejudice, bigotry, and narrow-mindedness, and many of our people need it sorely on these accounts. Broad, wholesome, charitable views of men and things cannot be acquired by vegetating in one little corner of the earth all one's lifetime." -Mark Twain

Without a doubt, serving our country has helped me grow into a more complete person and the words from this quote have proven true time-and-time again. My family might have been poor growing up but it's nothing compared to the poverty I have seen now. I have seen people in the worst possible situations keep a smile on their face and an open heart. I have experienced evil I never knew existed and watched the resolve of a human spirit to overcome it. And I have experienced love so deep that it transformed my heart and checked my ego.

These experiences have shifted my 1-10 life scale beyond the parameters I used to measure things in. If you are anything like me, you will discover how dramatically different experiences provide new highs and lows to consider. Also you will see how your old 1-10 extremes were maybe only about 3-7 compared to your new life scale. Travel, hardships and life experiences break your scale and create new measurements. So get out of your tiny corner of the world and see life for what it truly is.

Seeing another person's perspective

"What you see depends not only on what you look at, but also on where you look from." -James Deacon

Seeing another's perspective can be challenging, especially when we've locked in our ideals of moral or right. Furthermore, admitting that an alternate view has validity in a given situation can be an uncomfortable moment if you're not prepared to receive it. That's because these fractures break our thoughts from their settled foundations and expose our minds to unnerving change. However if you let it, this uneasiness can serve you by revealing a new point of view.

Alternatively, if you are attempting to challenge another person's perspective, be cognizant of your method. How you communicate matters just as much as what you are saying. If your delivery is condescending or actions brash, you are less likely to open others up to your message. Remember, a person's view of the world is formed through their collective life experiences. If you listen curiously and communicate respectfully, you might both gain unique vantage points to evolve your personal ideals.

Swing and a miss

"Believe in yourself and there will come a day when others will have no choice but to believe with you."-Cynthia Kersey

On a beautiful Ohio summer day, my family and I decided to have lunch at a local farm. Following the meal, we received free coupons to use at their entertainment area. Now normally my son would use his coupons for the big slide but that day, he and Grandpa got tokens for the batting cages instead. As petty as it may sound, when I saw him holding the tokens I got a little upset. Although we worked on hitting at home, in my mind he was only six and I didn't think he was ready for a batting cage.

I told him, *"Brother, you wasted those coupons. You could have ridden the big slide."* Unfazed, he said he wanted to do the batting cages, so I geared him up and sent him in.

Still I felt like he had no business being in there. Regardless, he believed all the work in the back yard prepared him for this moment, so off he went. With confidence, my little boy opened the cage, stepped in, inserted his token and stepped up to the plate ready to let it rip. As he missed the first five or six balls, I felt validated. I thought, *"He can't do it and he wasted his coupons!"* But just as I started to pat myself on the back, I heard him make contact. As I turned, I saw him hit another and another. Much to my surprise, he finished the round strong. Without skipping a beat, my little boy took his second token, put it in the machine and stepped up to the plate like a man. However, this round went a lot different. One ball after another went pinging off his bat. Solid contact and 8 of 10 sent back from where they came. I could not believe it! I remember standing there thinking, *"Wow, I put those limits on him yet he knew what he was capable of."* As he stepped out of that cage, I was the proudest Daddy in the whole place. I applauded him for ignoring my outlook and staying confident in his abilities.

What I failed to see in this moment was how my son's positive attitude and self-confidence were built on our training in the back yard. I, on the other hand, had a preconceived notion that he was too inexperienced and undeveloped for the battling cages. When he demonstrated his skills and confidence, he changed the way I saw him. Going forward, I learned to not make assumptions about another's capabilities based on my perception of their limits. I have also realized that if you spend time preparing your people and they have the right mindset, let them show you what they can do. Finally, when you get upset because you think someone is reaching too far or making a bad decision, keep it to yourself. Let them try, believe in their abilities and maybe you will be surprised like I was.

Promotion commotion

"Premature certainty is the enemy of the truth." -Nipsey Hussle

Have you ever had a sure thing slip through your fingers? If not, it's a heartbreaking moment that leaves you shocked for days or longer. One such moment happened to me when I was competing for a promotion. Before the process even started, I thought I was a shoo-in. Once I found out there was only one other applicant for the position, I believed my 50/50 odds shot up to 90/10. My overconfidence was supported by the fact that I was already a member of the organization, performing at a high level and having a positive impact on our new mission. With all these factors in my favor, I thought, *"If they don't hire me, obviously the other person would have to be so amazing that I could make peace with the outcome; but there's no way they'd choose this outside dude over me."*

Well as I am sure you can guess by now, when the time came, interviews were over and the decision was made, the leadership team chose the other applicant. Initially, their choice made me feel angry and unappreciated. I stewed for weeks, waiting for this new person to join the team. I fervently hoped he would be so impressive that I could understand their choice. Of course with the mindset I had at the time, no matter what this guy did or how remarkable he might be, I would have considered myself to be the better choice.

When I finally met him, I was in disbelief. He looked meek and seemed to lack almost every leadership quality I held in high regard. In my mind, they could not have made a worse choice if they tried. It was a total annihilation of my ego and fuel to my negative mindset. For months, I complained in secret, making jokes at his expense and looking for every flaw I could to single him out. My behavior became so destructive that I basically proved to the leadership team that they made the right decision.

Once I came down off my high horse, I began to search internally for the reasons I was not chosen. I asked for feedback from the hiring authorities, only to receive vague comments like, *"We just thought he was more ready for the position."* In response I thought, *"How do I work on my deficiencies with ambiguous feedback like that?"* Since their feedback was not specific enough to give me a direction, I delved deeper and paid very close attention to my actions around the work center. I began to recognize patterns that were caustic to our team and obstructed my ability to lead. I identified behaviors that were petty and unnecessary. I confronted my own emotions and learned to keep my useless sarcastic comments to myself. Only after opening this investigation on myself, did I start learning what being a leader was about.

In the months that followed, I decided to open myself up to new views and as a result, my behaviors began to change. I learned a lot from the guy chosen over me and began valuing different leadership styles. In the end, he became the Yin to my Yang. We simultaneously rubbed sharp edges off each other and I know we're both better off from our time together. Through that experience, I grew into a better person, team member and leader. Ultimately this occurrence taught me how a negative outcome can catalyze a positive change in our lives.

A tennis story

"If you are losing at a game, change the game." - *Gregory Benford*

Throughout my childhood, I was an athletically gifted kid. More often than not, I could throw, hit, shoot or kick a ball better than my peers. As I entered my high school years, my curiosity in sports grew and I decided to try a new sport, tennis. This sport was completely foreign to me but with my baseball background, I assumed I could figure it out.

During high school, my tendency to change sports created uncertainties about my athletic commitments. For this reason and our fiscal constraints, my first piece of tennis equipment was a wooden racket we picked up from the thrift store. As you might expect, practicing and competing with this ancient device made it exceptionally difficult to learn or win. However, after showing that I had real interest in the sport, my Dad took me to the store and bought me a $17 aluminum tennis racket. This change was transformational to my game. As I practiced and played with my new gear, I got much better but would still ultimately lose in competitive matches. As I thought about the reasons why, I conclude that my significant lack of formal training was to blame. In response, I decided to devise a strategy that appeared unusual to my opponents and utilized my strengths.

My advantages were a 6'3 frame, quick reflexes, strong arm and baseball skills. My plan was to start with a big serve, run up to the net and knock down any ball that tried to get by. If I had to use a forehand, I hit the ball as hard as I could at the body of my opponent. At the speed I hit, this made positioning their body and returning my hit fairly difficult.

After some practice and refinement with this strategy, I began to win. Eventually, I won the district championship and caused a bunch of rich kids to smash their $200 rackets into the ground.

What I learned from playing tennis was to not compete with my opponents on a level playing field. I lost when I played on their terms, so I created my own. To do this, I had to see and play the game of tennis in a different way. They had the advantages of formal training, advance technique and superior equipment. I had athletic ability, quick reflects, physical size and a chip on my shoulder. Since both sides were not equal, I had to tip the scales in my favor. To achieve this, I learned how to frustrate, confuse and compete with my opponents while still adhering to the rules. It was not the most eloquent style of play but it was effective and ultimately, it put me in a position to succeed.

If you are not having success with your current strategy, change it up. Look at your strengths and identify where your competition feels over confident. Push the boundaries and use unorthodox techniques that confuse or frustrate your opponent. Do not go toe to toe; go above, around or below!

Are you looking for flaws in the flower pedal?

"Stop looking for flaws and start looking for progress." -
Prachi Dash Mishra

When you read the title of this section, what did you think or see? Did you think about the statement, imagine the color, texture or beauty of a flower petal or did you automatically focus on the error? In this context, "pedal" should have been spelled "petal."

When someone presents you with an idea, poses a question or says something that challenges your way of thinking, do you keep an open mind or do you fixate on the tiny flaw? Are you able to view their thoughts as a 90% solution to your challenge or do you pop their balloon for the 10% that still needs work?

New ideas can be ugly at first. They are often presented in a moment and haven't been put through the rigor that smooths out their sharp edges. Throughout my career, I have worked at places where managers urged the workforce to come up with new ideas or innovative approaches, yet when an idea was presented, someone focused on the flaw and popped the balloon. In some cases, I was even personally chastised for not presenting a completely evolved and thought out idea.

This is not how we get the most out of our people or encourage initiatives. Let's listen to a person's viewpoint, see the picture they are trying to paint and work on the blemishes we find along the way. Prospect should be the aim, not perfection. So accept the flaws that come with new ideas and finesse them to their finale.

Bite sized beginnings

"The secret of getting ahead is getting started. The secret of getting started is breaking your complex overwhelming tasks into small manageable tasks, and starting on the first one." -Mark Twain

How do you approach your goals? Do you say, *"I'm going to work out for sixty minutes, three days a week?"* If so, how has that worked for you? If it has, keep up the good work. If not, I have an idea that may help you knock down the first domino. Begin with a bite sized action. If your goal was to eat an elephant, you'd get there one bite at a time, right? So why not try the same philosophy with your goal. Here's how I see it.

In order to meet your goal of completing a sixty minute workout, what's the first thing you must do? For me, it's waking up. So that's where I set my first goal.

*My goal is to wake up at 0500, three days a week.

What's the next thing you need complete before going to the gym? Getting dressed!

*My second goal is to have my workout clothes on no later than 0515, three days a week.

If you're up at the right time and dressed for the gym, what actions do you think will follow? My guess is you will probably head to the gym. Why? Because at that point it seems silly to not go! From there the dominos will keep falling.

So if you are having a hard time getting started on a goal, try initiating your process with a successful opening action. Build momentum with your second act and set things in motion to fall into place moving forward. Try this method or devise you own path; and if you haven't yet found what works for you, keep searching.

Let life change you

"We cannot direct the wind, but we can adjust the sails."
-Dolly Parton

How often do you purposely leave your comfort zone to push the boundaries of who you are? If you're like most people, it probably doesn't happen very often and that's why I believe life throws challenges our way. Throughout life, we get shoved into difficult situations that force us to make choices. I still remember coming home one day as a kid and realizing the lights had been shut off because we failed to pay our electric bill. I remember picking up aluminum cans on the side of the road to sell for cash. I can still take you to the grocery store that sold expired meat and dented cans. To this day, these memories drive me to be financially secure. I have lost loved ones, navigated two divorces, lost my hair due to an auto immune disease and have almost taken my life, yet I survived and am learning to thrive. Life has changed me. Sure, the lessons learned were hard but it made me the person I am today. I can now cope with stress in healthy ways. I can laugh at challenges and overcome them. I recognize hard times and know with confidence that the storm will pass, because it has a dozen times before. I let go of grudges because it takes too much of my energy and I forgive because I have been forgiven. Life has a way of presenting us opportunities to grow, just not always on our terms. So embrace life's challenges and let them change you. Chances are you will be happier with the person that comes out of the other side.

Question 1: What actions do you take to see something different?

Question 2: When is the last time you saw an issue from another perspective?

Question 3: What negative has triggered a positive in your life?

Question 4: Pedal or Petal and does it matter?

Question 5: How can viewing your goals differently help you achieve them?

Question 6: What life experience has changed your perspective the most?

LEADERSHIP CHALLENGES FOR TODAY'S WORLD

"In the end, it all comes down to leadership." -Ronald Reagan

The world has significantly changed over the last ten or twenty years and to effectively lead, our approaches have had to adapt. Opportunities to connect are ever present but new challenges have also emerged. So how do you lead in a constantly evolving world? How do you respect boundaries while utilizing technological advancements? How do you show appreciation and maintain an effective workforce? Well, hopefully you will find some answers and insights throughout this chapter.

Instant message does not mean instant access

"When someone oversteps your boundaries, they're letting you know what you want doesn't matter." -Phil Good

Over the last twenty years, technology has made

communication much simpler. It's made sharing ideas easier, coordinating actions more efficient and allowed us to stay connected with the people we care about most. It has revolutionized business and brought loved ones closer together. All in all, I think we can agree that these advances have been beneficial but I believe it has also allowed people and managers to infiltrate our personal lives.

For starters, I do not check my personal email every day, especially when I am on vacation, spending time with my kids or taking some down time for myself. Yet in some workplaces, I have been criticized for not responding to an email within twenty-four hours. What a message like that communicates to me is that I am not allowed to unplug from the world for a full day without checking some device or searching through my email. Furthermore, that some perceived "HOT" tasker takes precedence over my family time and spiritual/mental health. This does not set well with me.

So what do I believe is worth disturbing a person's downtime? Life or death circumstances, significant short notice opportunities and going to war! That's about it for me! However, since that is not realistic for all situations, consider what is appropriate in your organization. I would start this process by asking, *"If this was twenty years ago, would I have called that person on the phone or could it have waited until Monday?"*

As a leader, one way to reduce these intrusions is to establish communication routines and plan properly. If you create communication consistencies, your people will know when to check for messages. If it's genuinely urgent, follow up with a phone call or text to give your member a heads up. I implore you though; use this method as infrequently as possible. If you're always pinging your folks when the matter isn't important, you will become the boy who cried wolf. This type of frenzied behavior also highlights shortfalls in your management abilities.

I have a saying that goes, *"Your chaos is not my crisis,"* meaning don't rush me because you didn't plan properly. So respect people's boundaries, be reasonable on timelines and don't create crises when the situation isn't warranted.

Logical leadership dilemmas

"Logic will get you from A to Z; imagination will get you everywhere." -Albert Einstein

I believe modern day organizations have created a bit of a leadership issue for themselves. They've done this by hiring a disproportionate amount of people with logic based mindsets into leadership positions. Now, I am not saying that these people can't be good leaders but what I can tell you from my personal experience is a majority of these people seem to run risk averse, low empathy, micro-managed organizations. Furthermore, I have rarely met one who could see the big picture or paint a clear vision. Now don't get me wrong, I don't believe these people do this intentionally. Instead I believe that their inherent personality preference is to focus on logic based, detail driven decision making with low consideration for possibilities or human emotions.

As an example of this effect, I will draw on my experience in the Air Force. For a period of time the Air Force primarily commissioned people with S.T.E.M degrees into the Officer corps. I understand this train of thought, due to our evolving adversaries, uncertain warfighting domains and technological advances, yet I believe the idea of people leading people was lost in their considerations. I recognize that this group of people and the skillsets they possess are critical but at a certain point these folks will promote beyond technical work and their mission will become people. Pulling from my personal experiences, this transition is not an innate task for an engineer, computer programmer, scientist or mathematician. They overwhelmingly seem to favor the technical aspects of the job, the 1's and 0's and the grind. Dealing with complex human issues requiring extroverted actions or empathy tends to be unwelcomed work for them. I have seen this manifest itself in the form of apathy, delayed decision making, issue avoidance or analysis paralysis. In fact, this is one of the main reasons I believe some Air Force missions have become checklist driven. Because their leaders are science and math leaning, logical order, detail oriented people and checklists are a byproduct of that thinking style. That's not to say that checklists are bad, but when a checklist is the main tool for everyday actions, it creates an environment that stifles critical thinking. Remember, our young people are smarter, more tech savvy and creative than ever, so let's allow them to use these qualities to make us better.

Furthermore, generations of homologous personalities have created a reward and promotion system based on quantitative merits with very little consideration for qualitative contributions. Simply look at the forms, regulations and rules put in place and you will notice how difficult it is to capture the full impact of a qualitative action.

For example, how do you convey the impact of last minute babysitting during an emergency situation, taking care of a spouse while their person is deployed or lending an empathetic ear when a person is in distress? You can't because our system is not designed for those types of inputs. On numerous occasions, I have improved the lives of Airmen by knowing other people's stories and connecting them with people navigating similar struggles. As impactful as these moments have been, not a single one of them was used for promotion consideration or documented in an evaluation. In fact, most Commanders will probably never know about these contributions or how they led to higher morale within their organization and a more productive team. Once again, that's partly due to our system not identifying ways to account for such actions.

I say all that to say, make considerations for divergent people in your organization. Instead of hiring another person with a similar background to the masses, maybe consider someone who brings something different. Take time to identify what your organizational needs are and find people with the right experiences and personality types to complement them. If your mission needs to grow, find a visionary who can see into the future. If it needs to adapt, find a scrappy innovator. And if it needs technical prowess or standardization, find your technical person. Just do your best to avoid hiring one type of person at any level because as your people promote and missions evolve, you will need diverse thinking, experiences and flexibility to sustain success.

Finally, remember that different strengths are needed at different levels of management. Therefore, stay open to a person who may not check every box, give outsiders a chance and when you are faced with a tough decision, trust your gut feeling.

Do your mission effects, affect your rewards

"Focus on impact, not approval." -Tim Ferriss

Why do you reward people the way you do? Does it revolve around an expectation or excellence? Have you been doing the same old thing because that's the way things have always been done? I am convinced that reward programs are less about purpose and more about procedure. I have arrived at this opinion for several reasons. First, as I travel around and visit other units or businesses, I see outdated award boards all the time. If your boards aren't updated then my assumption is the recognition is not taken seriously. Second, almost every desk I approach in the Air Force seems to have a quarterly award on it. For me, it seems like these awards have become a Good Conduct Medal for your desk. Third, besides the supervisor and recipient, no one seems to remember who won the last round of awards. This tells me that the value diminishes quickly, therefore justifying the upfront work, time and frustrations that accompanies these programs is hard for me.

Maybe these aren't your experiences, but they are mine. If you share a similar opinion, ask yourself if there's a better way to show your appreciation. Furthermore, ask yourself what impact you are trying to achieve with your current methods and if it's effective at meeting its purpose.

Throughout my career, I have pondered the purpose of these programs and overtime have found an interesting division in the way recognition is presented. With this accumulated knowledge, I have concluded that it may come down to the affects you achieve in your mission? Are they "Kinetic" versus "Non-Kinetic"?

To illustrate my point, I will describe the two main reward categories in todays United States Air Force; Medals/Decorations and Quarterly/Annual awards.

A military medal or decoration is earned for outstanding achievement, meritorious service, acts of courage, etc... Basically, it's presented when you do something noteworthy. Additionally, it is not a rotating recognition program that seems to eventually result in everyone getting a turn. It is earned for action or sustained positive effort and its details are written up and placed into your permanent record. Finally, depending on the type of decoration you receive, such as an Achievement or Commendation medal, you earn points that help for promotions.

A military quarterly or annual award, in most cases, is also given when someone does something noteworthy. These awards have numerous categories and subcategories, making the pool of eligible people for each award fairly shallow. Often times, these awards are given to people who are exceling at their duties but at some locations they seem to have become participation trophies. The recognition from this reward lasts for a week or so, can be put into an annual evaluation for reference but does not carry with it any details or points toward promotion.

In my experiences working with the Army and flying world of the Air Force, I have noticed an overwhelming preference to reward outstanding individual actions with medals. Why? Because people in these mission areas are accustomed to delivering kinetic effects, meaning that they do things with specific, lasting outcomes in mind.

Take an Achievement medal for example. This reward type has a kinetic effect on the person receiving it. It gets them another point closer to promotion, it positively affects the rest of their career and it can be displayed proudly on their chest. It delivers a lasting effect. When people in kinetic mission areas recognize their folks for less noteworthy actions, it typically involves a memento such as a RMO/coin, inscribed hammer, dagger, or some other tangible object. This alternative award is always delivered with a firm handshake and a few meaningful words of appreciation. These physical awards are simple and do not require the time consuming efforts of a formal awards program. Also, from what I have seen, these tokens of appreciation seem to deliver the same personal effect as a quarterly award.

On the other hand, folks working in support mission areas seem to spend significant amounts of time writing up quarterly/annual award packages to recognize their people. For a majority of people, the impact of these awards consists of a temporary high, but seems to have very little impact on their career. I know there are some exceptions to this but as a general statement, I believe this to be true. Why? Because it has a non-kinetic effect, meaning in this case, that it has no lasting, substantial impact on that person's career. In many ways, this mimics their mission effects as well. Often times, support missions provide information or assistance to folks that execute an action. The product of their mission is typically non-kinetic until a kinetic capability takes possession of it. From my vantage point, I see the effect of a quarterly award as highly perishable. They don't go into your permanent record, they don't garner any promotion points and you can't wear it on your chest. Once the quarter is over and your picture is hopefully replaced, the accolades go away in addition to the award package that got you there.

From personal experience, the most I have ever derived from seeing a bullet referencing a quarterly award on an annual evaluation is the thought that this person might be above average and must have had a good quarter worth of work. It has never swayed my decision making paradigm because I formulate my opinions on what a person does once they join my unit, not what they did before I knew them. Additionally, when selecting someone for an opportunity, leaders usually engage in frank discussions and awards are rarely mentioned.

So why put more time, effort and money into an award when we could devote less time, money and generate a larger impact with a medal? Because I believe your actions seek outcomes you are accustomed too. Kinetic versus Non-Kinetic!

However, I'm not trying to say that quarterly/annual awards don't have a place. All I am asking you to consider is the impact of your reward system. Also, consider the impact on the person receiving it, if they prefer this style of recognition and if it's worth your precious time. If you believe a quarterly/annual award system is valuable to your organization, keep it going. If not, determine what serves your people best. Every time we turn around we're asked to do more with less time, people and money. So why hold onto antiquated reward systems if they aren't efficient or effective in this new normal? Adapt your rewards to meet your needs and achieve the outcomes you desire.

Cornhole Communication

"The single biggest problem in communication is the illusion that it has taken place." -George Bernard Shaw

Have you ever played Cornhole? If not, it's a game using two slanted boards with a small round hole in the top center and bean bags. To win you must throw the bean bag through the hole or at least land it on the board. Landing a bean bag on the board gets you one point but getting it through the hole gets you three points.

Now, think about the bean bag as your message and the hole as the optimal path for it to be received. Additionally, think of the board surface as all the possible ways to communicate with people, keeping in mind that every person has a unique way for receiving messages. If you are a traditionalist, you can aim for the standard top middle hole location but if the opening is not located there, the bean bag will never get through. Instead, change your aim to where the hole is on the board, not where you want it to be. And if you want to consistently win at this game, work on your delivery skills and learn to adjust your aim.

As leaders, it's on us to effectively communicate a message. If we only deliver our thoughts in ways that make sense to us, we risk excluding the people we need to perform a task. To communicate well we must remain flexible enough to use the platforms our people use. If they respond to text, reach out with a text. If they respond by phone, give them a call. If you know they aren't checking their email often, at least send them a message by other means to give them a heads up. In western cultures, effective communication is the responsibility of the transmitter not the receiver. So in today's world with numerous ways to communicate, tailor you message and delivery to ensure your message is received.

Holding people accountable

"Accountability. It is not only what we do, but also what we do not do, for which we are accountable." -Moliere

How do you hold people accountable at work and retain a work force when people have more options than ever? In today's low unemployment environment this task is a real challenge. For a person who takes feedback personally or believes you are too harsh, quitting and getting another job is quite easy. For many young people entering the workforce, I have seen professional feedback taken as an insult instead of an insight. They say things like, *"Well they just do not get me"* and keep bouncing from job to job until they find a place they think accepts them for who they are. I'm sure some never find that place. When receiving feedback, I think of Proverbs 10:17 which states, *"People who accept correction are on the pathway to life, but those who ignore it will lead others astray."* This short verse reminds me that correction is necessary as you strive for success and feedback isn't a step back, it's helping you take a step forward.

Furthermore, in our world of inclusion, participation trophies, and pats on the back, some people reaching adulthood do not understand that the world is made up of winners and losers. Over and over I have seen people who refused to be *"bossed around"* so they leave one dead end job for another. Oddly enough, this behavior has only resulted in them having even more bosses. What I think people should understand is that the marketplace does not need you. No matter how important you think you are, your work center will survive without you. We are all replaceable. If you are in a position that isn't mutually beneficial, move on. There's no need to be unhappy and the company probably doesn't appreciate having an unhappy employee either.

If you're a leader at any level in your organization, develop your standards, communicate them clearly and hold your folks accountable. If someone doesn't like it, they may not be a good fit and are probably not the kind of person that makes your team better, so let them go. The worst thing you can do is let someone drag the morale and performance of your team down because you refuse to hold everyone to the same standard. Not addressing an issue will absolutely cause conflict in a team. So maintain your standards, keep the right people on your team and chances are you will increase your likelihood of success.

An example of a modern worker

"Employees, especially young people, want more than a paycheck." -Marissa Mayer

A friend of mine has a teenage son who refused to get a labor intensive job, such as waiting tables. When asked why, he replied, *"Because I can do an easier job for the same amount of money."*

Initially, this was shocking to me. When I grew up, we took whatever job we could get. But now, the emerging work force does not feel the need to accept this rational and has become more analytical when deciding on a job. Paying your dues and hoping to get rewarded after some undetermined amount of time is an ancient idea for them. The modern work force has too many options to accept this paradigm. Instead, they are looking for meaningful work and responsibilities that help them grow. If you are having a hard time finding workers, you may need to increase your pay, benefits or advancement opportunities. Complaining doesn't help and sticking to the same compensation model you did ten years ago isn't going to cut it either. Find someone with a positive attitude, willingness to learn and an internal drive, and then compensate them fairly. Also, if you get a solid person on your team; give them ample opportunities to grow and develop them internally to become a valuable person in your organization for years to come.

The conflict between social media and mental tranquility

"Peace of mind arrives the moment you come to peace with the contents in your mind." -Rasheed Ogunlaru

People want mental tranquility yet their actions and habits don't support this state. So what's the conflict?

I believe that peace of mind is created through quiet reflection and meaningful conversations. If we continuously choose to stimulate our minds with new information, we don't give ourselves time to reflect on what we've already taken in. We enable this disturbance by filling our quiet moments with quick social media checks, thereby introducing new, sometimes inflammatory material into our minds. As a result, our minds lose focus on its current task and scrambles to make sense of the newly introduced information. Overtime, this continuous stream of stimulation locks our minds into an unending state of processing. I see it like the spinning Microsoft circle. However, if we allow our thoughts to process by ceasing our unrelenting inputs, maybe we can complete our cognitive tasks and better manage our mental resources.

So what am I saying? Stop picking up your phone and checking your social media feed at every stoplight, break or quiet moment. Take those precious moments to reflect in peace, process your existing thoughts and create small instances of mental tranquility. Just like your body, your mind needs time to rest if you expect it to perform at its best.

Sharing is daring

Giving coworkers and subordinates access to your personal life though social media is risky and can potentially make carrying out work responsibilities more difficult. Sharing our opinions, views or associations on social media can create unintended consequences in the work place. Here are some examples of social media content I have seen impact people in the work center.

Political statements or affiliations, religion, lifestyle choices (sexual, personal style, piercings) and hobbies such as; Live Action Role Playing, Dungeons and Dragons, burlesque style dancing, etc...

When you choose to share those aspects of your life with co-workers and subordinates, you open up an opportunity to connect or invite conflict into your relationship.

To avoid tricky situations, I would advise against friend/follow requesting someone you supervise or who is in your chain of command. It can make things awkward if that person chooses to not accept your request because they prefer to keep their personal life out of the limelight of their leadership team. Additionally, they may feel obligated to accept your request because of your position in their professional life and that's not a fair position to put them in.

If your subordinate friend/follow requests you, either accept it or go have a talk with them about the reason you haven't approved it. Nothing is more awkward than not knowing why you are specifically excluding them from your personal life, especially when other coworkers may already be connected with you on a platform. Either way, be careful when mixing your personal and professional lives. It only takes one comment or picture to create a situation you did not expect and change a relationship you worked so hard to nurture.

Question 1: What's important enough at work to disrupt your family/personal time?

Question 2: What type of person does your organization need at this time?

Question 3: What affect are you trying to achieve with your reward system?

Question 4: How adaptable are your communication methods?

Question 5: Think through something you saw on a person's social media page and recall how it affected your opinion of them.

JUST BECAUSE YOU DON'T THINK YOU DID ANYTHING WRONG, DOESN'T MEAN YOU DID ANYTHING RIGHT

"An attitude of accountability lies at the core of any effort to improve quality, satisfy customers, empower people, build teams, create new products, maximize effectiveness, and get results." -Tom Smith

Have you ever met someone so indifferent about a situation that they avoided responsibly for the result? Where does this come from? How can we justify turning the other direction when we see something wrong? How are we able to disconnect ourselves from an outcome we could have changed? In this chapter we'll explore how our inaction or apathy impacts the world around us.

Inaccurate evaluations

"People are more inclined to pass the buck than they are to take responsibility. The fact is, though, passing the buck doesn't build your character or give you the opportunity to learn from your mistakes." -Marshall Goldsmith

Have you ever been given an assessment or annual evaluation you know you didn't deserve? Better yet, have you ever given someone an evaluation that did not accurately reflect their performance? All too often I see supervisors "check the box" of their assigned duties by giving their subordinates a cookie cutter, uninformative, vapid report. However over that same evaluated period, I heard them comment, complain and seek advice on how to handle their subordinate's behavior. So why don't they just capture this truth in the evaluation? I'll provide my opinion in the sections below.

When an evaluation is falsified, my first inclination is the supervisor failed to remain engaged with their subordinate over the rating period. The title of "Supervisor" carries with it a responsibility to provide feedback thereby, allowing those in your care to understand their deficiencies and make adjustments. Failing to perform these duties on a consistent basis can highlight a supervisor's irresponsible conduct. Therefore, to prevent any conflict or confrontation, the supervisor covers their tracks by giving out high marks on an evaluation.

For more attentive supervisors, I believe avoiding conflict or an uncomfortable conversation gives rise to the number of inflated reports. I understand this part of the job is difficult for some but if you want the financial compensation or title that comes with supervisory roles, you need to learn how to have honest conversations with your people.

And of course, some supervisors are just lazy and decide that giving their subordinates high marks will shield them from having to do any real work as a "leader." This scenario is completely unacceptable! By not doing their job, these supervisors are denying their member key pieces of information that could help them grow. Additionally, not representing your person accurately potentially takes away opportunities from others who earned high marks but are now having to compete against people that don't deserve it. This apathetic inaction hurts both the individual and organization over time.

Case in point, during the first half of my military career, my supervisors failed to give me the ratings and feedback I deserved. I was frequently lauded for my hard work but clearly lacked tact and possessed numerous rough edges that could have used some rounding. Yet, all I ever heard from my supervisors was, *"You are doing a great job!"* and *"Keep up the good work!"* As a result, I kept repeating the same behaviors. After years of success, one day deep into my career I finally received my first evaluation mark down. I still remember the impact it had on me. At first I couldn't believe it, but at the same time I could. My supervisor marked me accurately, had a conversation with me and it forced me to look at my behaviors in a whole new light. Years later, I was arguing with one of my first supervisors on a ridiculous social media post and he dropped in the fact that he did me a favor by giving me high ratings I did not deserve. This made me furious! All along he knew what I needed to work on but instead he took the easy way out. I thought of him as a coward. I responded by telling him he failed me. I told him that he should have marked me accurately so I could have started working on my deficiencies sooner. Maybe then I could have been a better leader in the earlier parts of my career. In my opinion, that would have been the real favor!

Conversely, most evaluations I have written over my military career contain accurate markdowns or ratings. Some folks are initially upset when they see this but once we sit down and have a conversation, they understand the rating better. Additionally, I make it a point to ensure regular feedback is given throughout the year, so once we talk things through they usually aren't surprised. Once the air is cleared and the member understands the specific reasoning and advised actions to resolve this mark, they often appreciate the fact that I took the time to mentor, explain and assist them in their development. The funny thing is more people have thanked me for a marked down evaluation than for a perfect rating. I think it's because they recognize the value of good feedback, respect an honest conversation and leave our meeting with a tangible goal in mind. Perfect evaluations are not a call to action for your leadership development; it's more of a pat on the back and positive reinforcement that you accept every behavior they portray. However, honest markings and clearly communicated feedback will drive your people to advance their skills and improve their intangibles.

Delegation alone is not empowerment

"Delegating doesn't mean passing off work you don't enjoy, but letting your employees stretch their skills and judgement." -Harvey Mackay

How many times have you been "delegated" a task that in reality, someone else just didn't want to do? They tell you it's some opportunity to excel but in reality you're just dealing with a booger that's been flicked your way.

If you are in a position of authority and are going to delegate responsibilities, you need to make sure the recipient has a basic understanding of what is being asked of them.

Telling someone to complete a task without knowledge or basic skills is a poor use of their time and energy. Moreover, this haphazard approach will likely cost you time and energy you didn't account for as well. At a minimum, you should ensure that the assigned person has received documentation to refer to, a clear picture of what you are looking for and any forms, phone numbers or other resources they may need to complete or start the task. If you take the time to set them up for success, it's more likely that learning will be achieved on their side and time savings on yours.

To provide some clarity on how I see this scenario, here's an example to think through. One night after a long day at work and making dinner, you tell your ten year old kid to help out by doing the dishes. Before that day, they have never washed or dried a single dish but in that moment you decided to delegate this responsibility to them.

Now how would you expect this to go? Would you expect them to know how to complete this task to your satisfaction without being shown how to do it first? Do you think they inherently know how to load a dishwasher, add soap and turn it on, even if they have seen you do it a few times? What if all of the dishes don't fit? Would you expect them to hand wash the rest? Do they know where to find the sink dish soap and drying towels? If they run out of soap, is it ok for them to notify you or is there some other way you would like them to acquire the resources they need to complete the job? Do they need to put the dishes away after they are washed or do you just want them washed? What's your guidance?

Do you see how delegating this task of doing dishes is not empowering to a ten year old kid? Chances are they will be confused and the outcome will likely fall short of your expectations. These same principles can be applied to delegating tasks at work. Don't just assign a task because you're tired and don't feel like doing it. You can almost guarantee a subpar result. Instead, gradually prepare your people to take on duties as they demonstrate their capacity to climb. Ensure that your expectations are clear and they are equipped to handle most variables if they arise. Of course, there will always be a learning curve when a task is delegated, but if you do your part as a leader it is more likely that they will achieve success and feel empowered in the process.

What's the intent?

"What is the quality of your intent?" -Thurgood Marshall

Knowing a person's intent is important when handling tough situations. I believe for the most part, people act with good intentions but sometimes lack the skills or methods to achieve their desired outcomes. To keep this positive perspective at the forefront of my mind, I internalize the words of a friend who says, *"Always assume noble intent."*

As an example, reflect on an unhappy past or present coworker. When asked to express their opinions, they typically respond with a negative comment or indifferent attitude. When prompted to provide feedback, their underlying tone reeks of sarcasm and criticism. One of my favorite go-to words for these people is *"Actually."* Next time you're in a room with a person like this, listen and see if you hear a comment that sounds like, *"Actually, the training wasn't that bad."* Or, *"You know what; he actually did a good job."* To me, using the word *"Actually"* in this context gives the impression that you expected something to go poorly but were surprised when it went well. To the person receiving these words, this expression communicates that you had low expectations of their work but were satisfied with the outcome, this one time. If you are a person who inadvertently uses this word, I recommend you find another way to express your thoughts. People see a compliment with *"Actually"* in it to be backhanded and insincere.

Before we go on, I want to be clear that I am not defending negative people. I recognize why these folks have earned their bad reputation and how they affect a work center but after reading this section, I'll ask you to reconsider their attitude. Why? Because, I have learned though my encounters that when confronted about their attitudes, they usually have a valid reason. This experience has helped me see them differently. By sitting down and talking with them one on one, I often I find they care deeply about the issue they are acting out against. In most cases they "actually" want to help fix it. You may think this is naivety on my part but I feel this way because at one point in my career, I was this person.

Almost daily, I saw issues that frustrated me, areas where we could improve and red tape to be cut through. As I identified the issues and saw no action to rectify them, my irritations grew. What might have been constructive comments at the beginning eventually deteriorated into snarky statements and sarcasm. I sincerely wanted the situation to improve but I allowed frustrations to drive my communication.

As I have reflected on this period in my life, I have realized that my methods to communicate these concerns were not only juvenile but also ineffective. For some reason, I thought highlighting these issues in a sarcastic or humorous way would bring more attention to them. I assumed that once the issue was brought into the light, our leadership team would recognize the problem and seek solutions to fix it. In reality, my actions were ill received, causing me to become an ineffective leader. Because of this, I earned a reputation as a negative person, people dismissed my plights and I lost some capabilities to care for my subordinates. After a while, it seemed like every time I went to bat for my people, I could watch the leadership team's mental eye roll taking place. Of course, this was the exact opposite outcome I was going for and it led to even more dissatisfaction and disgruntled behavior in the workplace.

Instead, what I should have done was keep my public, sarcastic, juvenile comments to myself. They never seemed to help and it just sowed seeds of frustration amongst everyone else on the team. Second, I should have worked directly with the people responsible for the programs, processes or personalities at the root of my problems. Once I gathered more information with them, we could have discussed realistic expectations or possible solutions. Finally, in a leadership role I have learned that remaining optimistic when issues arise is a mainstay behavior. Chances are everyone who needs to know about a given situation is already aware and it's not okay for leaders to publically or privately fuel the issues with our negative comments or actions. As leaders, we need to stay focused on solutions and keeping our subordinates focused on "Can do" areas. These "Can do" areas are spheres of influence in the work center where a person can take ownership and accomplish tasks. If we can keep them focused on these influential areas, we can give them a path to fulfillment as opposed to frustration.

To avoid negative comments and keep my frustrated outbursts in check, I have developed a metaphor to illustrate how I see navigating aggravations in the work place.

Forest Fire

To begin, imagine you are in a large forest that has been set ablaze. As you look around, you see fires of varying sizes and intensity. In this illustration, the forest is your work center and the fires are all of the personal and professional issues you encounter throughout the day.

Now imagine that it's your job to extinguish these fires but you have only been equipped with a large backpack full of water and a hose. For most of us, we are limited in our resources to combat the issues we face at work. Some issues are just too big to solve on our own. Therefore, we must be judicious in our effort and deployment of resources to ensure an effective outcome.

Once you've accepted that you're resource limited in this fight, you'll learn that you need to let some of the smaller fires burn out on their own. If you choose to address every fire you see, you'll run out of water resources for the fires that truly matter. By observing the environment, understanding what makes a fire burn, what fuel is needed to increase its intensity and where to best apply your water, you become more effective at controlling the situation. If you cannot accept letting certain fires burn out on their own, I would encourage you to look around your work center for those people who try to address every issue. Then tune into how people around them respond to their comments. Chances are you will see that people label them as complainers and you'll recognize how their words have lost power. As we grow in our leadership roles, we need to learn how to focus on the issues that matter and how to apply our efforts and resources effectively.

One or two will do

I think we can all agree that constructive feedback is critical to our growth stories but what happens when you receive too much at once? I know for me it can feel a bit overwhelming and disheartening. When someone presents me with a "constructive" feedback laundry list, I sometimes receive it as a list of things I suck at! Then in the wake of our interaction, I have a tendency to feel overwhelmed and either take their feedback personally or feel confused on where to start. What's my biggest flaw and is there something I should be working on first?

As a leader, neither of these situations is how I want to leave an interaction. This result is unlikely to achieve the intent of my efforts and by creating a sense of frustration or making a person feel overwhelmed, I may cause them shut down during future engagements. So how can I approach this task in a better way? By only providing one or two areas of suggested improvement at a time.

When you only give one or two pieces of feedback at a time, the person receiving it tends to feel less beaten up by the interaction. Additionally, they won't see your inputs as an insurmountable list of weaknesses but will hopefully envision a manageable goal to work towards. Only giving one or two pieces of feedback during an interaction can also help you keep a focus on the positive side of things. Compliments for things they did well and speaking words of encouragement over them will stick more if they aren't left feeling hammered by your conversation. Remember, too much criticism at once can steal the intent for your guidance.

If you find you have a list of areas you would like your subordinate to work on, keep it for yourself and once they succeed at fixing one item, slowly introduce another.

However, don't always have something in the chamber ready to unload once they complete a step in the right direction. Give feedback at a leisurely pace and recognize that you may not be able to address everything you want to in the time you have with them. You need to be ok with that! If you do part ways with your subordinate sooner than you would have liked, you want them to remember your time together fondly. It is better to say good-bye with them feeling supported than to get in all your criticisms and leave them feeling discontent.

Handling trash talk

"Don't worry about those who talk behind your back, they're behind you for a reason." -Autumn

Some people don't see an issue with talking trash in the work place. For some, this behavior has become so common that its existence has been accepted without understanding the full impact it has on an organization. This perception is especially true in work place cultures where these actions are not addressed or confronted. So how do you confront a person about this behavior? I start by asking, *"What's the intent behind your comments?"* or *"What are you seeking to achieve by bad mouthing this person?"*

To do this effectively, you need to make sure you are in the right state of mind to ask these questions and listen objectively. Upon initial reflection, a person may realize their intent is hurtful and stop this behavior on the spot. In other cases, the person might have a legitimate grievance and you need to be open to hearing their thoughts. If the issue is with you, be open to changing your ways or explaining the reasons for behaviors they dislike. Feedback without change is disheartening and knowing why someone is frustrated can be disarming! If they are taking issue with someone else in the organization, discuss better ways to handle it and how these behaviors can be harmful to the team. The one thing you cannot do is allow this behavior to persist.

A Rock in your Shoe

"Let go of the attachment, keep the lesson" – L.J. Vanier

Sometimes we carry people in our lives that slow us down. I've held on to burdensome people due to loyalty, hope and sometimes selfish personal need. However, as I've faced hard decisions in my growth story, I've accepted that we need to let some people go. This action isn't done with ease but is necessary once we discover that some people keep us from reaching our full potential.

To help me understand the impact of weighty personal attachments, I've developed a metaphor comparing these relationships to having a rock in your shoe.

When a rock gets in your shoe, it might not bother you much at first. You might shift it around for a bit or pretend it's not there but eventually if you choose to not remove it, you will experience discomfort. If you are walking, the rock steals your attention and keeps you from enjoying the intended purpose for your stroll. If running, the rock becomes a constant distraction and slows down your pace.

So why don't we just remove it? I think we all have our own reasons for that! However, keep in mind that you have the power to remove the rock at any time. You don't need permission from someone else to take off your shoe and the rock doesn't get a say! It's your choice when and how you part ways with this nuisance.

With that being said, recognize when someone is causing *"A hitch in your giddy-up"* or for you city folks, slowing you down! You choose whether to hold on knowing they cause issues or deciding to free yourself from their hindrance and move forward at your own pace.

Silence and inaction are choices

"Injustice is not always associated with action. Usually it is in an inaction." -Marcus Aurelius

How do you react when something shameful occurs? Do you stand up for the afflicted or stroll by without intervening? Some would say these situations are, *"None of my business"* but what if your instincts tell you something isn't right. Is it ok to overlook the situation? My answer no! Now I am not saying you have to go put yourself in the middle of a fight or uneasy predicament but I believe you should find a way to distract, deflect or deescalate an incident. If none of these are possible, at a minimum you should contact the authorities. Don't wait for someone else to intervene. That's why you are there. When you choose to remain silent at a moment of injustice, your silence is an action. Maybe you don't think you did anything wrong by sitting on the sidelines, but I would say you also didn't do anything right!

Question 1: Why are inaccurate evaluations harmful to your subordinates and organization?

Question 2: How can you better prepare your people for delegated tasks?

Question 3: What's one situation when your intent and other people's perceptions were not aligned?

Question 4: What fires can you let burn out on their own?

Question 5: How can you better handle trash talking in your workplace?

Question 6: Who is/was the rock in your shoe? Why are/were you carrying it?

USE COMMON SENSE TO GET THE JOB DONE

"Common sense in an uncommon degree is what the world calls wisdom." -Samuel Coleridge

Do you find the more time you spend around people, the more you realize that common sense isn't that common anymore? Sometimes I feel like humans make processes more difficult on purpose. Even in simple daily interactions, I see employees who feel so constrained by policies, regulations or procedures that they refuse to use their internal problem solving skills on basic issues. Instead, they align themselves with words on a piece of paper and tell the human being standing right in front of them, *"I'm sorry. There's nothing I can do to help."* Why is that? When did we stop using simple problem solving skills to care for our fellow man and instead give policies authority over our natural instinct to solve people problems?

If you are a company or organization that doesn't empower their workers to solve people problems, you're doing it wrong. Whatever it is! People are what buy your products, travel on your airplanes, and request your services.

Furthermore, if you are in a leadership position, what common sense steps are you taking to allow people to get their jobs done? Are you calling meetings just to hear yourself talk or exercise some authority over your people; or are you finding work center solutions and searching for ways to make your processes more efficient?

Using common sense to get the job done

"It is common sense to take a method and try it. If it fails, admit it frankly and try another. But above all, try something." -Franklin D. Roosevelt

On a trip home from six weeks of military training, I landed at a small, two terminal Midwest airport at approximately 11:30 p.m. on a late December night. Our arrival time was earlier than expected, causing everyone aboard to be in an upbeat mood. This positive development was even more welcomed since most of us were weary from the long travel day and anxious to reunite with our families for the Christmas holiday. As the plane pulled off the taxi way and into the gate area, we all began to anticipate our inevitable exit. As the plane came to a stop, our seatbelts unbuckled like an ensemble of poorly tuned instruments and we all stood up to grab our luggage and unload. Chatter picked up as a sense of joy and relief washed over the cabin. This long day was almost over and now all we had to do was grab our luggage, hug our loved ones, catch a short ride home and crawl into bed; or so we thought! After standing there motionless for about five minutes, the flight attendant came onto the loud speaker and announced that the sky bridge was malfunctioning. She followed her statement by saying a mechanic had been called out to resolve the issue. At the time, this seemed like a trivial hiccup and hardly worth getting irritated over. After all, we arrived early and from the sound of it, this was a minor issue that would not take long to fix. After another five minutes, she came over the intercom again and told us that they were still waiting for the mechanic to respond. Another five minutes went by and again we received the same explanation.

Finally, over fifteen minutes later she told us the mechanic had arrived and was looking into the issue. Hooray, we thought! The end was in sight. But as we sat there waiting in these late night hours, many of us looked out of our windows and couldn't help but notice several open terminal gates around us. An initial scan showed the two gates next to us were clear and at least another six were open within one-hundred yards. As the word began to spread about the open gates surrounding us, some of the other passengers and I started discussing the idea of just moving to another gate. After all, it was almost midnight on a Friday and this airport was dead. As a consensus formed, we suggested having the person just inside the gate walk down about twenty-five feet and open a gate on either side of us. It shouldn't take long or be that difficult, right? For many of us, this seemed like a quick fix to expedite our departure and allow the airline to keep their customers satisfied. As we vocalized this idea to the flight attendant, we only received assurances that the sky bridge issue was being resolved.

To the passengers, it seemed like the crew failed to consider any of the possible solutions around them. For them, fixing the sky bridge became the priority and emptying a plane full of increasingly frustrated people became an ancillary goal. A common sense approach would have focused on emptying the plane, getting people on their way and providing the best possible experience in the face of inconvenience, right? Well, this could have easily been achieved by moving one gate over. Instead the crew and ground team affixed blinders for the single obstacle in front of them and lost sight of the main objective.

Finally, after about one hour of trying to fix the sky bridge with a plane full of passengers sitting ten feet from the exit, they finally moved us to another gate. The resulting interactions with the crew were fraught with frustration. Based on what we had just experienced, I got the impression that the airline had not empowered their crews to think or devise solutions on their own. This ultimately resulted in transforming a plane full of happy travelers into a mob of irritated people. Simply pulling into another gate or bringing out a staircase to enter the airport through another door could have resolved this matter in minutes. However, in spite of these simple solutions, the airline team opted to stay the course to the detriment of their customers and reputation.

My take away from this experience was to stay committed to your objective, not the means in which you get there. It did not matter if we offloaded from that gate, another gate or a staircase. The goal should have been getting us off the plane safely and on our way. Sometimes you will face obstacles on your journey. Don't get stuck at the roadblocks. Find a way around, circumvent challenges with a common sense approach and focus on completing the mission!

Learn how to ask

"Asking a question is the simplest way of focusing thinking...asking the right question may be the most important part of thinking." -Edward de Bono

Have you ever had someone ask you a question without really knowing what they wanted? They might say something like, *"Tell me everything you know about the competition,"* without understanding how complex an answer can be. Consequently, you look confused because the question is so broad you're not even sure where to start. In response, you ask a series of additional questions to figure out what they mean and how to get them the answer they desire, such as; *Are you asking about established competition? Emerging competition? Do you want to know about a specific product or service the competition provides? How much detail do you want? How much time would you like spent answering this question? Etc...*

When someone asks me broad question like this, I compare it to a consumer interaction at Baskin Robbins. In this scenario, you are the employee and the person asking a vague question is the customer. When the customer steps up to the counter, you can assume they want ice cream, although every once in a while they choose a sherbet option just to keep you on your toes. In this analogy, a poorly worded request from a customer might sound something like,

"Hello, I would like some ice cream!"

To which you reply, *"Great, you have come to the right place! What kind of ice cream would you like?"*

A person who knows what they want might say, *"Chocolate Chip!"* and you ask how much, give them the requested flavor in the amount they want and send the satisfied customer on their way.

However, all too often the requestor doesn't know what they want so when you ask, *"What kind of ice cream would you like?"* They might respond, *"Just ice cream!"*

You counter with, *"Well, we have thirty-one flavors to choose from, which one would you like?"*

To which they respond, *"I do not care, I just want ice*

cream."

In this story, the thirty-one flavors represent all the possible answers for their question. However, since they do not know exactly what they want, you may have to start making some assumptions. This is an inefficient use of your time and will likely result in a dissatisfied customer as well.

So in an attempt to move this transaction forward and give the customer what you think they might want, you scoop out some Black Walnut ice cream, extend your arm over the counter and hear, *"Oh, sorry! I'm allergic to nuts and I don't like this ice cream."*

Then you go back to trying to help this person again. *"Well, what kind of ice cream do you like?"*

To which they reply, *"I do not care; just give me anything without nuts!"* So you try another flavor and get another negative response.

This guessing can obviously go on for a while or you can stop wasting your time, and start asking clarifying questions to figure out what the customer actually wants.

You, *"Do you like Chocolate?"*

Customer, *"Well yes!"*

You, *"Caramel?"*

Customer, *"No!"*

You, *"Marshmallows?"*

Customer, *"Nope!"*

You, *"Mint?"*

Customer, "Yes."

You, *"How about some Chocolate Chip Mint ice cream?"*

Customer, *"That sounds delightful!"*

In my experience I have learned that if someone asks you a broad or complex question like this, don't try to answer it in the moment. Instead if possible, respond with an invitation to sit down and talk through the question and what type of information they are searching for. Briefly explain to them that the question they asked is complex and to efficiently use your time and get them the information they want, you need to better understand their request.

If you get the same general questions time after time, build some informative products that can be updated and delivered to requestors. If your scope is much larger, build a twenty questions type template that helps you get to the root of a request faster. If this method can work for figuring out random thoughts in a game, it can work for your questions as well. In my experience this tactic has been quite useful for distilling broad topics in our semi-limited work life into easier to understand requests. Whatever you do, build some common sense methodologies to make better use of your time, create happier customers and help the work center run more efficiently.

Look to leverage all available resources, even if they aren't yours

"Innovation is seeing what everybody has seen and thinking what nobody else has thought." -Albert Szent-Györgyi

At times, do you feel like you're scrambling around while others are just cruising through the day? I have found this often occurs as responsibilities shift from one team or person in an organization, to another. So how can you adapt and overcome the initial surge? Look to leverage all available resources, even if they aren't necessarily yours.

As an example, at one of my units we underwent a period of extreme growth. We had new people joining our sister unit almost daily and before long they maxed out all of the available training classes. The subsequent backlog created a pool of underutilized, smart, energetic people who were excited to make meaningful contributions in their new unit. On our side, we had growing requirements that went unfulfilled due to a manning shortage of qualified people. After some discussions with the other unit's leadership team, they agreed to let us use the new folks to help with mission related tasks before they left for training. This was a great win-win for both organizations. They needed experience in the mission and the mission needed research and aggregation done for specific tasks.

To capitalize on this manning resource, I invested four hours of my time training two classes of new people. With about twelve people now trained and using about four hours a week of their time, I received around forty-eight hours in additional manpower to accomplish our mission. To emphasize this point, my single four hour training investment generated twelve times more man hours every

139

week for the foreseeable future.

Additionally, I learned through their research, gained new perspectives from their thoughts and built relationships with our newest cadre. This instance ended up being a great opportunity to fulfill mission needs, utilize available resources and develop new people while establishing a baseline foundation for success.

Conversely, some people get so caught up in their own whirlwind that they perceive efforts like this to be a waste of time and instead try to do everything themselves. Speaking from extensive experience I can assure you, you don't succeed by pulling a train on your own. Had I tried to take on this task without their help, my effort would have fallen woefully short and I would have been unable to deliver quality products to our customers. Instead I used an available resource to meet the demand and grow new people in our mission area.

In another instance, my section lost our work spaces as our building sought to accommodate a new unit worth of people. However, we still had to get our jobs done without the proper resources. So how did we overcome this issue? We utilized some old laptops found in storage, the skills of our people in another section and a seldom used side room, to set up an internet café. It was not a permanent solution but it allowed us to get our work done with limited resources and space.

So when faced with a challenge, keep an eye out for opportunities. There always seems to be a few hanging around. Throwing your hands up or pretending you have no options isn't going to solve your problem. So get creative and start looking for less obvious solutions.

Put people before paperwork

"Organizations do not get things done. Plans and programs do not get things done. Only people get things done. Organizations plans and programs either help or hinder people." -Admiral Hyman G. Rickover

Has anyone ever put a company policy, regulation or process before your well-being? How did that make you feel? Did it feel like they got so caught up trying to comply with a piece of paper that they forgot about the person standing right in front of them? I recognize there is a purpose behind these structures but in some cases a policy, process or regulation doesn't make sense for a given situation. One of the most agonizing interactions to watch is when people with a genuine need get stone walled because of a process.

In one case, I saw an old Veteran come into a building that previously had a finance customer service area. The service counter was shut down a while back and the only means to receive assistance for finance issues was to submit a help desk ticket through the accounting system website. As the Veteran searched for someone to help him, he came across a young Airman working in the finance section and asked for his help. After hearing the Veteran out, the young Airmen replied that he would need to go online, create an account and submit a ticket through the system. The Veteran replied, *"I don't have a computer and I don't know how to use one."* As the conversation continued I almost couldn't believe what I was hearing. This Veteran needed help and the Airman's solution to the problem was to repeat the same answer over and over again. At this point, I chimed in asking the Airman take this Veteran back to his desk, help him create an account and show him how to submit a ticket. This ticket would then go directly into the queue of the Airman, and he could resolve the issue that day. Fortunately, this

Airman took my suggestion and the thankful Veteran was able to get his pay issues resolve.

My point is, when you have the ability or flexibility to solve an issue, find a reason to assist, not resist. Regulations can become outdated. Processes can be over burdensome. Policies are not written to cover all circumstances. Look at your individual scenario and find a path to help someone out.

Additionally, if a policy is outdated or an issue arises, bring it to the attention of your leadership team. If possible, have a discussion and see what you can do to get it recanted or modernized. Saying things like, *"That's just the way it is"* or *"It is what it is"* is not an acceptable answer. Although you may have to adhere to a process for the short term, if it involves unnecessary steps, work to change it for the betterment of everyone. Believe it or not, managers don't want inefficiencies in their teams or processes. Most are looking to maximize the efficiency of every member and make their customers happy. If you can make a case about how this improvement will result in efficiencies, I imagine you would be successful in making a change. Finally, if your leaders or managers are reluctant to change, seek to understand the intent for the process and look for new economical ways to meet your objectives.

Are you a simple saboteur?

"Nothing is less productive than to make more efficient what should not be done at all." -Peter Drucker

Does there seem to be a lot of red tape in your organization? Have you created inefficiencies, sought to eliminate them or just adhered to a process because that is the way things have always been done? Is there a better way to complete an action using a common sense approach?

Once you read this section, I will ask you to take a serious look at how your organization conducts business. That's because what you are about to read comes directly from the *17 Jan 1944 Central Intelligence Agency (CIA) Simple Sabotage field manual.* This document was specifically created to outline ways of sabotaging the effectiveness of an organization. The crazy thing is for many of you, what you are about to read might sound all too familiar. Here is an excerpt of this twenty page document but I would encourage you to read it in its entirety to understand its full effect.

https://www.cia.gov/news-information/featured-story-archive/2012-featured-story-archive/CleanedUOSSSimpleSabotage_sm.pdf

(11)General Interference with Organizations and Production

(a) Organizations and Conferences

    (1) Insist on doing everything through "channels." Never permit short-cuts to be taken in order to expedite decisions.

    (2) Make "speeches," Talk as frequently as possible and at great length. Illustrate your "points" by long anecdotes and accounts of personal experiences. Never hesitate to make a few appropriate "patriotic" comments.

    (3) When possible, refer all matters to committees, for "further study and consideration." Attempt to make the committees as large as possible-never less than five.

    (4) Bring up irrelevant issues as frequently as possible.

    (5) Haggle over precise wordings of communications, minutes, resolutions.

    (6) Refer back to matters decided upon at the last

meeting and attempt to re-open the question of the advisability of that decision.

(7) Advocate "caution" Be "reasonable" and urge your fellow-conferees to be "reasonable" and avoid haste which might result in embarrassments or difficulties later on.

(8) Be worried about the propriety of any decision; raise the question of whether such action as is contemplated lies within the jurisdiction of the group or whether it might conflict with the policy of some higher echelon.

(b) <u>Managers and Supervisors-</u>

(1) Demand written orders.

(2) Misunderstand orders. Ask endless questions or engage in long correspondence about such orders. Quibble over them when you can.

(3) Do everything possible to delay the delivery of orders. Even though parts of an order may be ready beforehand, do not deliver it until it is completely ready.

(4) Do not order new working materials until your current stocks have been virtually exhausted, so that the slightest delay in filling your order will mean a shutdown.

(5) Order high-quality materials which are hard to get. If you do not get them argue about it. Warn that inferior materials will mean inferior work.

(6) In making work assignments, always, sign out the unimportant jobs first. See that the important jobs are assigned to inefficient workers of poor machines.

(7) Insist on perfect work in relatively unimportant products; send back for refinishing those which have the least flaw. Approve other defective parts whose flaws are not visible to the naked eye.

(8) Make mistakes in routing so that parts and materials will be sent to the wrong place in the plant.

(9) When training new workers, give incomplete or misleading instructions.

(10) To lower morale and with it, production, be pleasant to inefficient workers; give them undeserved promotions. Discriminate against efficient workers; complain unjustly about their work.

(11) Hold conferences when there is more critical work to be done.

(12) Multiply paper work in plausible ways. Start duplicate files.

(13) Multiply the procedures and clearances involved in issuing instructions, pay checks, and so on. See that three people have to approve everything where one would do.

(14) Apply all regulations to the last letter.

(c) Office Workers

(1) Make mistakes in quantities of material when you are copying orders. Confuse similar names. Use wrong addresses.

(2) Prolong correspondence with government bureaus.

(3) Misfile essential documents.

(4) In making carbon copies, make one too few, so that an extra copying job will have to be done.

(5) Tell important callers the boss is busy or talking on another telephone.

(6) Hold up mail until the next collection.

(7) Spread disturbing rumors that sound like inside dope

What did you think? How many of these actions do you see in your organization today? If these were written specifically to sabotage an organization, shouldn't we be seeking to eliminate these actions from our work centers?

Reading this document has given me insight into bad

habits we have developed in our organizations over time. It also helps me focus on common sense approaches to daily tasks and reminds me of how inefficiencies impact an organization. Now that you know how these behaviors effect an organization, what can you do to eliminate their existence?

Question 1: What situations have you faced that could have been resolved with a simple solution?

Question 2: Are you committed to a method or an objective?

Question 3: How can you ask better questions or provide better answers?

Question 4: What available resources do you see but have not asked to use?

Question 5: How have you been affected by policies? How can you put people first?

Question 6: What actions from the CIA Simple Sabotage field manual do you see in your place of work? How can you eliminate them?

WHAT I WISH I KNEW WHEN I WAS YOUNGER

"Learning is the process whereby knowledge is created through the transformation of experience." -David Kolb

Here is some mid-life advice from a guy who has experienced a bunch of anxiety, setbacks and consequences due to ignorance or lack of perspective. I hope it gives you some insight and peace of mind for your stage in life.

Stop comparing your life to others

"The reason we struggle with insecurity is because we compare our behind-the-scenes with everyone else's highlight reel." -Steven Furtick

Social media has a way of making us feel like our life is either incomplete or lacking. For some, this feeling drives you to compete with other people's lives. I used to get triggered when a friend showed off something I wanted, went on an amazing trip or constantly posted pictures of their perfectly constructed designer life. However, what I have learned is that these calculated outlets to the world are self-produced illusions. Knowing the back story for some of these people helped me realize how rarely their public persona reflected reality. In many cases, their behind the scenes life consisted of severe debt, strong feelings of discontent and an unhealthy need for the approval of others. Very rarely did I see someone's life be as glamorous as they portrayed it on social media. So, if you are trying to compare your life with others, stop! You do not have all the facts or insights to compare your lives equally, so at the end of the day you are just wasting your time.

Another factor to keep in mind if you are comparing your life to others is that their life situation may look very different than yours. They may not have kids, spent years living within their means or prioritized things differently than you. Furthermore, each person's objective in life is different and our definitions of success vary widely. Simply put, we are all running our own race. Therefore seeking success over someone else is like trying to win a race you aren't even running.

Moreover, stop trying to live the life of someone ten or twenty years older than you. So often I see people in their early twenties trying to emulate the life of a middle aged person. Why? Live in your season of life. When in your early twenties, you aren't supposed to have all the things a person with two more decades in the workforce has accumulated. The nicer house, higher trim level car and stuff older folks have comes from decades of hard work and good decision making. If you want to get where they are, go ask them how they did it. Additionally, to gain a realistic perspective, ask them what their lives looked like at your age. Often times I have found they were in a similar place to where you are right now. Once you learn their secrets and identify their pitfalls, chart a path for yourself, be patient and let the process unfold over time. Trying to keep up with the

Jones' is only going to hurt you in the end.

Our experiences were meant to be shared

"Sharing life brings the greatest joy." -Lailah Akita

Why are we so quick to share our positive experiences but keep our negatives ones in the dark? They both have value, yet we put up a facade and only reveal the happy few. I believe this behavior keeps us from building connections with people.

When I was younger, this was my style. I always felt the need to hide the valleys of my life and highlight the hills. As a result, I missed out on opportunities to connect with people and help those who were struggling with familiar situations. However, as time has passed I have realized that our experiences were meant to be shared. As a reminder, I have developed the following analogy.

Do you know why the Great Salt Lake is so salty? Because, water flows in but never out. Most lakes have an outlet, but not the Great Salt Lake. And since there is no outlet, minerals have concentrated over time and made the fresh water bitter.

Conversely, rivers move both good and bad substances downstream. They don't hold onto to minerals because they know it's needed by others along the way. They have visible signs of their past experiences but still freely share the resources that come their way.

Experiences are like minerals in water. They are beneficial in the right dosage but can become toxic if held in. We were meant to come in contact with them, take what we need and pass them on. Holding onto them makes us bitter.

Having an outlet keeps us healthy and brings life to those who are down river from us. So don't hold your life experiences in, open your waterways and allow the gifts of your experiences to flow into others.

I'm gonna ain't getting you anywhere

"Take action! An inch of movement will bring you closer to your goals than a mile of intention." -Steve Maraboli

How many times has someone told you they were gonna do something only to never see it through? I'm gonna go back to college when I have time. I'm gonna make a career change. We're gonna have a kid when we're ready. I'm gonna get in better shape. Well guess what? I'm gonna ain't getting you anywhere.

To begin, procrastination is arrogance. It conveys that your timeline is more important than everyone else's. By putting things off to the last minute, you make an assumption that you can scramble to success, inconvenience others or delay your life's purpose to a time of your choosing. Then when things don't come together like you hoped, you make excuses or blame others for missing an opportunity. To be clear, you are to blame if you haven't prepared your life to receive a blessing.

I compare people who say they're gonna do something to a tentative person who's too afraid to merge into traffic. Instead of moving forward, using the merge lane and finding an opening, they just sit there and wait until all the conditions are right. Well if you don't know this already, life is traffic that never stops! There isn't a perfect condition. You just have to find an opening and get moving in the right direction. If you're too afraid to move and get in the flow, you will probably be sitting there for a while, watching as people pass you by.

However, if you are willing to move out on faith in the direction of your goals, I have found that life adapts to your new circumstances. Once in the midst of the mayhem you develop a new path that guides you to your objective. In fact, I know people with three kids and a full time job that grind toward completing their college degree. If they can do it, you can do it.

You will never be ready for your first kid, so don't be fooled. Travel and enjoy your life while you're young but don't put a time table on having kids until you think you're ready. For some, that day never comes and those who wanted a family but were too concerned about the "what if's" end up watching those around them live the life they wanted.

Getting and staying in shape is an everyday thing, so no need to wait for this goal. All you gotta do to get started is choose something healthy at your next meal, decide to take the stairs instead of the elevator or pick a parking spot farther away to ensure you get in those extra steps. Big immediate actions like joining a gym or buying massive amounts of vegetables you won't eat isn't necessary to get started.

If you are stuck in one of these *"I'm gonna"* cycles, how do you break the trend? Maybe this will help!

D.E.C.S (Decide, Execute, Consistency, Succeed)

<u>Decide-</u> Make a decision and visualize the outcome. I have found that for some, making a decision is the hardest part of the process. However, once the decision has been made and the path is set, the task of getting on with it seems

much easier. Once you decide and visualize, you will understand what you're going for and have an idea of what a successful result will look like.

Execute- Execute actions in support of your decision. If you're gonna get in better shape, you will probably need to change some habits. When I'm trying to get back in shape, I start by holding myself to the "Taking back 1%" rule and focus on executing on my 100.8 minutes each week. This gives me the flexibility I need each day to get in my 14.4 minutes and enough room to make up time at the end of the week if life events throw off my schedule.

Consistency- Being consistent is by far the hardest part of this process. Life has a way of putting obstacles in our path but if you can find ways to get back on track, you will find success. I also use the "Taking back 1%" rule to keep me consistent in my actions. To get my 100.8 minutes in a week, I need to be consistent or I will be left with large amounts of time to make up on the weekend. Remember, "Taking back 1%" of your time is not a selfish act. It enhances your life so you can be better for those around you.

Succeed- If you make a decision, execute actions and stay consistent, success is almost inescapable. By using this simple process, I am confident you can reach your goals. Additionally, I believe you will find people along the way to propel you forward, help when you reach a roadblock or join you on the ride. People on the pathway to success create their own gravity and before you know it, the right types of people will start coming into your life.

The necessity of check and balances

"Nature has introduced great variety into the landscape, but man has displayed a passion for simplifying it. Thus he

undoes the built-in checks and balances by which nature holds the species within bounds." -Rachel Carson

Do you know what happens when you remove necessary elements from an ecosystem? It gets out of balance.

In the 1930's people viewed wolves as a nuisance in Yellowstone National Park. To resolve this issue, people eradicated wolves from the ecosystem allowing other more desirable animals like elk to thrive. As a result, the elk began pushing the limits of Yellowstone by consuming young plants needed by other animals to survive. Additionally, the impact of an unchecked elk population led to increased erosion and a significant decline in populations of beavers, fish, birds and other species in the park. In 1995, wolves were reintroduced to Yellowstone and many of the issues caused by the oversized elk population have been resolved. The wolves have kept elk on the move, allowing young plants to take root and grow. They have reduced the elk population down to healthy levels and species that were on the verge of disappearing are making a comeback. Criticized and undervalued, wolves still have their opponents among some ranchers, hunters and residents around Yellowstone. However, this small population of enforcers has successfully prevented elk from destroying the park and helped restore a more balanced ecosystem for all.

In my opinion, what happened in Yellowstone is occurring in our modern military. When many of us came in, you were bound to come across some crusty old Sergeant that kept you in check and off the "Commanders grass". This distinct population held people at all levels accountable and refused to take excuses for obvious inadequacies. As a result of this declining faction, I have noticed a tangible change to the military culture.

One indication I see when visiting other units is the apparent ruts worn into the grass and abundant weeds framing the front of a building. The exterior does not express pride and because of government contracts, so many of these locations don't feel empowered to remedy their situation. As frustrations about this transparent issue are raised, I have watched Commanders tell the old crusty Sergeant who is trying to assemble a team to correct this problem, to stand down. The enforcer has been silenced.

When we switched from starched uniforms to wash and wear, I remember being so excited. I thought, *"Now I don't have to waste my time caring for this uniform."* But as a result of the switch, I have noticed a sense of pride in professional appearance subside. No one has to put effort into their uniform when they wash and wear it. Additionally, back in the day you would have never gotten away with a subpar appearance. Everyone looked sharp and the anomalous dirt bag uniforms were promptly handled by a supervisor or some crusty old Sergeant. Now if you try to iron a crease or starch that knife edge through your stripes, people rebuke you. Once again, the standard seems lowered and the role of the enforcer is diminished.

Finally, if you speak too directly you are labeled as insensitive or out of touch. To clarify, I am not talking about people who are outright mean or petty. That behavior is not acceptable. I am talking about direct people who tell you the hard truths but are unfairly characterized as being mean. I think this flavor of people and their derived interactions are just as important as empathetic leaders with huge hearts for their people. However, it seems like these people are harshly criticized for speaking uncomfortable truths to people who need to hear it most.

The changing role of the Sergeant is not a bad thing but I

believe the slow elimination of the enforcer function is hurting our military ecosystem. Although viewed as a nuisance in our ever progressing world, this role has a necessary place in our work centers and especially in our military organizations. It keeps people on their toes, creates an uneasy environment for inattentiveness and demands that boundaries be respected and standards be upheld, or a price will be paid.

As a young Airman, I disliked these folks. They called me out and demanded I maintain the standards. From my perspective, they were just angry, unnecessary people. However, I also remember making sure my stuff was squared away once they checked me on it. They impacted my behavior. Now I see how enforcers keep an ecosystem healthy and afford the right amount of uneasiness to keep the majority in line. It may not be the most glamorous role but in my opinion, they are a key element for an organizations ecosystem to thrive and a vital check and balance.

Put the matches away

"Sometimes you get the best light from a burning bridge." -Don Henley

If there was one thing I would go back and tell my younger self, it would be, *"Don't go around burning bridges."* At multiple jobs and assignments I have learned how my past actions affected my future opportunities. It's a bit embarrassing to explain past behaviors to co-workers and people who know you by your notorious reputation. Trying to convince people that you have changed, grown or matured every time you reunite in a professional environment is a bit exhausting as well.

I have taken time to do an in-depth analysis of my

historical behaviors and when combined with my personality type, I think my excuse for these past actions was me, *"keeping it real."* I decided sugar coating wasn't for me and I was going to always speak directly and unfiltered. I never consider how to effectively communicate my thoughts to people that were not like me. Instead, I often opted for the bull in the china shop approach. This behavior built me a solid reputation as a jerk and made working with me undesirable. Additionally, as I started paying attention to the wake I left, I realized that these behaviors and my reputation negatively affected my ability to get things done for my subordinates. There is something called good rapport and I was in short supply with the people I needed help from the most.

If you are reading this and feel like you might be this type of person, just know you can only go so far alone. At some point you will need help from other people and I hope you have built good relationships if you expect to get anything done. On the other hand, if you choose to keep throwing people under the bus and being unpleasant to work with, I imagine you will go through the same challenges I found down that path. So good luck!

The solution is evolution

"Evolve or dissolve…It is your decision." -Larry Price

If you want to continually succeed in life, you should remain open to change and new ideas. Consider this, animals have learned to evolve over thousands of years. They have adapted to new environments, survived diseases and out smarted predators. The ones that didn't are extinct. That's because they didn't evolve to solve for changing elements in their environment.

In our personal and professional lives, we have to evolve as the world around us changes. We can't decide who we are in our twenties and then maintain all the same habits, behaviors and attitudes through our forties. It's just not realistic. Some of the most frustrated, angry, unsuccessful people I have ever met are defiantly inflexible. They say things like, *"You're not gonna change me!"* or *"No one is going to tell me what to do!"* or *"That's who I am, you need to learn how to deal with it!"* As I have watched these people careen though life, they seem to collectively end up in similar circumstances; bouncing from job to job, looking for someone who "gets" them or stuck in the same old miserable place without opportunity for advancement. If you don't evolve as you mature and transition through professional stages, climbing the ladder is going to be hard. Our lives and careers are ever evolving environments and the best way to survive or thrive is to stay flexible and adapt to the changing world around us.

As you evolve in life and develop your leadership philosophy, you will find solutions for issues that once plagued you. Are you having a hard time getting to the next level in your career? Old friendships slowly dissolving? Relationships not growing with your needs? These issues might result from your resistance to change. As you mature, your desires will likely evolve. If you're hitting a wall, it might be because you have chosen to maintain habits or behaviors that keep you from advancing to the next level. Maybe you're holding onto a relationship that no longer serves you well and need to let that person go. Or maybe you have finally realized you can be more than you thought possible. If you want to achieve your new definition of success, you may need to make necessary changes to alter your surroundings and create beneficial relationships. Whatever your situation, be prepared to evolve if you want to reach new heights in life.

Remain teachable

"Experience teaches only the teachable." -Aldous Huxley

Life is a never ending cycle of teachable experiences. Some are good, some are bad but all are educational. As I have aged and experienced more of what life has to offer, I have learned a few key things I would like to share with you.

First, never assume to know everything about anything. For every so called expert I have met, I have come across several others more informed than them. Be cautious when referring to yourself an expert because others might seek to humble you or assume you are not open to learning.

Second, listen with intent when you feel like tuning out.

Third, recognize that every perspective on subject is an opportunity to refine your understanding of it.

Most importantly, sometimes the lesson is not in the content but in the experience itself.

When I was twenty-five, I can remember thinking I had life figured out. I didn't listen to others very well and I couldn't wait to chime in with my wisdom on a topic. When people said something that didn't align with my views, I dismissed it and label that person as an idiot. I was insufferable at times and so arrogant that lesson after lesson passed me by. In reality, as time has gone by, I have discovered that I know very little about life. To drive this point home, life has sent me transformational experiences over and over again. Now I understand that learning never ends and the moment you think you've got something figured out, a humbling experience is probably on its way. Also, I seek to learn from every situation and accept that everyone has something new to teach me.

If you are young, ask questions and carefully listen to the answers. Bounce your perspectives off others to refine your views of the world. Be receptive to new ideas and constructive feedback. Find mentors that think differently from you. And above all, go into every situation with a teachable spirit.

Question 1: What impact has comparing your life to others had on you? Was it time well spent?

Question 2: What is the "I'm gonna" in your life? How can you get started?

Question 3: What check or balance is missing from your workplace ecosystem?

Question 4: What is an area in your life that needs evolving?

Question 5: Are you open to teaching or focused on preaching? Why?

DON'T ABSORB TITLES

"Think twice before you speak, because your words and influence will plant the seed of either success or failure in the mind of another." -Napoleon Hill

People give us labels all the time. They call us crazy, stupid, lazy, fat, distracted, angry or any other term they feel describes us in a moment. Depending on our behaviors or condition at a given point in time, these remarks might be accurate but that doesn't mean they define who we are. If you absorb these words as your truth, they can become seeds in your soul and weeds in your self-image. However, if you refute these negative statements, you can choose to only take in titles that build you up and nourish your inner being.

Box of Rocks

"You never know how long your words will stay in someone's mind even long after you've forgotten you spoke them." -Unknown

Growing up I would say I was a curious and adventurous kid. You could find me jumping off the garage with a black garbage bag parachute, climbing way too high in a tree or playing with poisonous snakes. It was just the kind of kid I was! But as I did these things, some of the influential adults in my life thought my actions were dumb and gave me the nickname, "Box of Rocks." This was meant to signify that I was dumber than a box of rocks.

Initially I didn't think much of it but as time went on, others began calling me this name as well. After hearing this nickname repeated over and over again, I started to absorb it. I can clearly remember thinking I was stupid and accepting mediocrity as my passage in life.

This nickname also gave me an excuse when things went wrong and it became a part of my identity as I traversed my adolescent years. Each time they would say, *"Boy, you're dumber than a box of rocks!"* they got a good chuckle out of it, but for me it stirred up internal questions about my intelligence, curiosity and adventurous personality traits. It also made me wonder if I would ever be smart enough to do something meaningful with my life.

As I grew older, I fully absorbed this title and it stuck with me. Going into my professional life I thought I lacked the intelligence to be successful. When I met people that sounded intelligent, I was intimidated. Instead of being vulnerable enough to ask questions and learn from these people, I became defensive and tried to pretend I already knew what they were talking about. My pride and insecurity caused me to miss out on so many opportunities.

This perception of dimwittedness is pervasive in my family. On many occasions I have heard my father refer to himself as a dumb person. As a child, when you hear that coupled with inputs from other influential adults in your life, you start to believe it as your truth as well. I have thought on numerous occasions that being dumb was part of my genetic makeup; that I just needed to accept this deficiency as a reality in my life. However, as I have broken down self-imposed limits I have learned that being dumb is not my inheritance and stupid is a title. I decide who I am and I can change any label I want. So that's what I did.

As you will see later in this chapter, this wasn't easy and others were not helpful either. However, eventually I shed this moniker and started believing in my God given gifts.

Air Force Academic Award

"The problem with the world is that intelligent people are full of doubt, while the stupid people are full of confidence."
-Charles Bukowski

Going into the Air Force was more of a scramble than a plan. After failing to do anything meaningful at two colleges, having a car accident that left me without transportation and no real prospects, I went to an Air Force recruiting office and choose the first decent job available. When asked what I wanted to do, I told the recruiter, *"Something in radio."* I had always wanted to work in radio, running the sound board and making music. As he searched through the options, he came across a job that had radio waves in the description. Not knowing any better, I thought it sounded interesting. As he described the job, he named off some odd sounding equipment like oscilloscope. I convinced myself that it was a piece of equipment at a radio station and was sold.

Remember young ones, in the time before smart phones and the entire internet was in your pocket, when someone you trusted told you something, you took their word for it. As I would find out about four months later, I had selected a career field that was way out of my comfort zone. See, I fancy myself as an English and History kind of guy. I had always done better in these subjects and was comfortable learning them. Conversely, the military job I choose was all Science and Math. Like all of it! It was a rude awakening when I showed up a tech school and didn't see a single radio station or familiar piece of equipment around.

As the course started, I felt my insecurities grow. I had already convinced myself that I was not the kind of person who understands these subjects or could do this type of work. I had a defeated spirit within the first week. In the weeks and months that followed, I did my best to keep my head above water. However, the information was so different and new that I had no way to create common links in my brain. I had to learn from scratch and it was my worst nightmare. By the grace of God, I got out of there with a B and anxiously waited to see what my first assignment would hold.

As fate would have it, I was selected to go to the most technical, Math and Science filled assignment you could get out of tech school. All of the things I disliked during training would be presented daily and I was not excited. My tech school lasted about four months but the training timeline at this assignment was another six months of even more in-depth technical training.

Every day at my new assignment was a grind and the people training me didn't make it any easier. If you didn't understand a concept, they would mock you. If you couldn't remember or complete a formula, they ridiculed you. It was as if they wanted you to know how smart they were, how dumb you were and any time spent with you was a waste of their energy. Their tactics made you shrink and feel like you couldn't ask questions without consequences. All you wanted to do was pass the next section and expedite the process so you wouldn't have to spend time with people who intentionally made you feel inadequate every day.

After completing the training, their comments and sarcasm persisted. Never was an opportunity missed to publicly shame you for making a mistake on an assignment. It definitely was not a learning environment. Over time I studied and worked hard to guard myself from their comments. As I grew more knowledgeable, I started to gain confidence and their comments lost their sting. After a while, I knew I was on par with them or at least approaching that status.

Then I found out that once a year I had a chance to prove myself in an academic competition. It was called Sensor Olympics, a service wide academic test to show where you ranked in your job knowledge. For our career field, this meant working long mathematical formulas without a calculator, converting units in scientific notations and solving complex problems by hand. Months later when the results came out, I was notified that I finished #2 in the Air Force for my career field. The company I shared the top three with was impressive and better known throughout the community. However, for me this moment was an opportunity to shut my critics up. I finally had undeniable proof that their words were hollow and my aptitude was real.

After I not so humbly told and showed them I was smarter than them, they never spoke another word about my intelligence again. Later, when I became an instructor for this subject, I tried to avoid using words and attitudes that made people feel stupid in a learning environment.

I tell this story not to brag but to describe how I overcame my stupid title for the first time in my life. I was tired of people telling me who I was, so I set out to change their minds and my own. After I earned this recognition, I never heard people call me dumb again. And even if they did, I finally had self-confidence and a new label none of them could claim. This win set me on a path to earn two college degrees and earn the first undergraduate degree in our family, with honors.

Garbage in, Garbage out

"What you feed your mind determines your appetite." - Zig Ziglar

What you allow into your mind creates your perception of reality. Just like feeding your body the right foods makes it healthier, feeding the right things to your mind creates a healthier mindset as well.

I believe most of us grow up with unhealthy self-talk. Some of us got these views from others but us lucky few were able to create them for ourselves. However, what I find interesting about our self-perceptions is how we hold onto labels even after we've evolved out of the situations that created them.

For example, through my adolescent years I accepted titles that were given to me such as stupid, fat and weird. Since these were not enough, I personally added incapable, lacking, unlovable, outsider and outlier. Each one of these words is tied to some moment or series of events that I used to convince myself of their validity. As I have gone through life with this mental hindrance, I have gotten into the habit of describing myself to others in these deprecating terms.

In my professional life, I have sabotaged interviews and first impressions with phases like, *"I'm not the smartest guy you will meet but what I lack for in brain I make up with effort."* This comment typically garnered a confused look on the other persons face.

I still occasionally refer to myself as a fat kid. It's like I see my current good health as a temporary state and I'm giving my future self an excuse to relapse into the shape I was in over twenty years ago.

I have called myself incapable so I could create off ramps when a task becomes challenging. It's an easy out and I can prove my truth with negative speak to myself. And on more than one occasion, calling myself incapable became a self-fulfilling prophecy.

So why do I do these things? Because I have been these things! However, what I have come to realize is that I do not reflect these labels anymore. To fight this negative self-talk, I have started taking account of my achievements.

To combat my stupid label, I think about my academic awards and two college degrees. I have also received numerous compliments from peers and students about my intelligence and ability to simplify complex problems into digestible ideas.

To push against my fat kid label, I look to my almost unbroken record of "Excellent" PT scores over a military career. I also take note, and a little joy, when I run past someone who is in visually better shape than me. Who knows if they just finished a marathon but it gives me a little boost to brighten my day.

Incapable has probably been my most difficult label to contest. Jumping into something new like a language, musical instrument or business venture can be daunting. In the past I have viewed these endeavors as vulnerabilities for not knowing something, but now I choose to see myself in the empowering state of learning.

State of Mind creates State of Matter

"In everyone's life, at some time, our inner fire goes out. It is then burst into flame by an encounter with another human being. We should all be thankful for those people who rekindle the inner spirit." -Albert Schweitzer

The state that you, your matter exists in right now is created by your state of mind. How you act, function and endure is a direct result of the energy you have put into your life, through your mind. See, your mind is the catalyst that changes your state of matter. It's the Bunsen burner supplying energy to activate physical reactions and energize our molecules. Our minds are the instruments that enable us to change our matter from one state to another. Before we go on, I will describe our four states of matter and how I think they look in our lives.

Matter exists in four natural states. Solid, Liquid, Gas and Plasma.

Solids are relatively inflexible. They have very low kinetic energy and the particles do not move much. They have defined shapes and do not conform easily to their environment.

My desire is to never be a solid. I believe to be the best possible leader in a changing world, remaining flexible and having energy is vital to meeting the new challenges we face. To stay out of this state, I try to keep an open mind, read books that give me perspective and stay flexible when unfamiliar changes come into my life.

In a liquid state, particles have more room to move and

are flexible. Liquids have some kinetic energy. Matter in this state has an indefinite shape and will conform to a container it's put in.

Being in a liquid state is my minimum standard. To stay in this state, I work to gain knowledge and perspectives that help me remain flexible in my thinking. In a liquid state I can also conform to my surroundings if needed. However, one of the problems I have with liquids is that they fill containers from the bottom up. To me, this signifies that their reach is limited and only touches the easiest to fill spaces of the environment they are in.

In a gas state, particles have a lot of space and high kinetic energy. Gas has no definite shape or volume. If unconfined, the particles will spread out indefinitely; if confined, gas will expand to fill its entire container. When gas is put under pressure by reducing the volume of the container, the space between particles is reduced and the gas is compressed.

My goal is to remain in a gas like state if I can. Matter in a gas state has lots of energy and can spread out across large areas. When gas is confined to a container, it completely and evenly fills the space, reaching every surface of its borders. Additionally, compressed gas is constantly pushing against its boundaries in an attempt to go further and further.

Plasma is not a common state of matter here on Earth, but when you see it, you can tell right away that there is something different about it. Stars are essentially superheated balls of plasma. Plasma consists of highly charged particles with extremely high kinetic energy. The noble gases (helium, neon, argon, krypton, xenon and radon) are often used to make glowing signs by using electricity to ionize them to the plasma state.

When you see someone in a plasma state of matter, you will know it. These people burn brighter than the rest of us and can be the spark that initiates change in our minds. If you need something to kick off a phase change in your life, find a person in plasma and figure out what makes them glow.

Going through phases

We all go through phases of matter but it's important to understand how or why we are in our current one. The basic concept to keep in mind is that, as we add or remove energy from our matter it causes us to change from one phase to another. When we apply heat to our lives, our particles become energized. When our substance reaches a high enough temperature, our solid becomes liquid, liquid turns to gas and so on.

Conversely, when we don't generate heat or allow it to be removed from our matter, our particles slow down and begin to settle in one spot. When our substance reaches a cool enough temperature, high energy gas state becomes a liquid or liquid becomes a solid.

In life you are either adding or removing energy from your matter. The longer you stay cold, the harder it will be to transform your state. The more you read and learn, the more you will turn the heat up in your life.

Lisp lecture

"Never argue with stupid people, they will drag you down to their level and then beat you with experience." - *Mark Twain*

Just before one of my Professional Military Education

course graduations, a senior leader pulled me aside and suggested that I not deliver the graduation speech. His concern was that public speaking may not be my forte because I had a lisp. To him, this made me unqualified to talk to a room full of people. Before this moment I had briefed Distinguished Visitors, General officers and auditoriums full of people. Of course, I knew my lisp was there but up to that point, no one had ever tried to take an opportunity away from me for this minor speech impediment.

As his words settled in, I remember feeling insulted and getting snippy about the whole thing. I assured him that I could handle the moment and after a while I think he just felt so bad about his comment that he let me do it.

When speech night came, I decided to adlib portions of my comments, just to make him feel uneasy. I had the microphone and he was helpless to stop it. I did a few extra toasts as well, just to get everyone in the right "spirits." When he confronted me after, I dismissed his comments. All I could think was, *"Screw you buddy!"* How petty was this guy; yet I acted pretty petty as well. Since then, I have worked on my lisp and feel comfortable with it is existence. Additionally, I have taken every opportunity to speak in front of others and refine my public speaking skills to the best of my abilities. I refused to accept his outlook on my capabilities and it has pushed me to seek more speaking roles in my life.

Successful mind fields

Just like a farm, successful mental balance is achieved by preparing the soil, planting seeds, nurturing plants, harvesting the bounty and resting the fields.

Step one: Prepare the soil.

This is done by softening the ground, removing rocks and abating weeds in order to create successful conditions for planting. For your mind, prepare yourself to receive new thoughts, ideas and information by loosening your firmly held beliefs and mitigating cognitive impurities.

Step two: Plant high quality seeds and vary the crop.

If you use poor quality seeds to sow your fields, you will likely achieve subpar results. Additionally, if you plant the same crop year after year, overtime your fields will underperform and pestilence has an opportunity to establish itself. For your mind, find sound materials that lend new perspectives and help you grow. Vary your content, rotate your focus, prevent stagnation and learn to create conditions for enduring mental health.

Step three: Nurture the plants.

Nothing grows without proper conditions, nutrition and care. For your mind, nurture the ideas that take root. Feed them with supporting information and develop a holistic viewpoint so they can thrive.

Step four: Harvest the bounty.

Plants don't exponentially grow and varying seasons drive the harvest. In farming there is a time to reap and sow. Farmers plan for these the best they can! For your mind, reap the knowledge you've sown when the seasons of your life begin changing. Put away the harvest you've produced and it will serve you well during the winters of life.

Step five: Rest the fields.

Everything needs rest. A field needs rest to restore its nutrients and structural integrity. For your mind, give yourself a mental break from time to time. Move from a state of collection to a period of reflection. Things break or destabilize when they are pushed beyond their limits. Even God took the seventh day off! So accept periods of rest and let them prepare you for new production when the time comes.

Success is not final, failure is not fatal

"Failure is not the opposite of success, it's part of success" -Arianna Huffington

I do not see successes and failures as destinations, but as journeys. They are both temporary states that can change. Just because you had one win or shining moment doesn't make you a success. Same goes for failure! Failing at one thing doesn't make you a failure. I have chosen to not absorb either of these titles. Instead, I have decided to accept the title of "Determined". To me, this signifies that I am still pushing to get better and will not be defined by setbacks. As I have read and learned about our most celebrated industrial leaders and inventors, I have found that every one of them had numerous failures leading up to their eventual success. What sets them apart was being determined, so I will be that!

Another trap I try to avoid is telling people who I used to be. As Les Brown says, *"Used to be's do not make honey!"* I interpret this to mean that what you did in the past is not the thing that produces results today. If someone asks who you are, tell them who you are today and own who you have become. Whether you have failed or succeeded in your past, do not rest on those outcomes. See where you want to be and describe yourself by where you are going!

Question 1: What titles have you absorbed?

Question 2: What proof do you have that confirms you are no longer that title?

Question 3: What are you letting into your mind?

Question 4: What is your state of matter?

Question 5: How can you activate your mind and generate heat to change this state?

CONSISTENCY IS KEY

"Success doesn't come from what you do occasionally, it comes from what you do consistently." -Marie Forleo

Consistency in all aspects of your life will determine your outcomes. The habits you etch into your daily routine generate your mindset. The people you surround yourself with create your environment. Your choice to practice constructive behaviors will reap results. The same principles can also negatively impact your life. Consistently choosing to not exercise or eat right will become detrimental to your health. Deciding to watch TV night after night will keep you from pursuing more fulfilling purposes. Whether good or bad, your life will be defined by the consistency of your choices and actions.

Consistency in your surroundings

"Walk with the wise and become wise, for a companion of fools suffers harm." -Proverbs 13:20

Who you surround yourself with matters. Have you ever heard the saying, *"Your income is the average of the five people you spend most of your time with?"* Well, I believe this to be true and I have noticed my drive, income and viewpoints change as my inner circle has evolved. To demonstrate how my outlook has changed, I will walk you through my journey.

I grew up in a lower middle class neighborhood in Fort Worth, Texas. The people there were kind, friendly and hardworking. Growing up in my neck of the woods, work ethic and consistency were the tenets of success. The overarching hope was that if you stuck with your job and were lucky enough to avoid layoffs, you would receive a decent paycheck and maybe a nice little retirement in your latter years. It is a respectable way to live but is also fraught with apprehension and fear. Why? Because when you live from paycheck to paycheck, you're always one unaccounted for expense away from disaster. As a result, your life becomes centered on hoarding resources (money, bulk groceries, material possessions, etc...) as you wait for the hammer to drop (layoffs, setbacks, family emergencies).

As I reflect on those times, I would compare our view about money to that of a short sighted squirrel. In this story, a squirrel sets out to store enough acorns for the winter. Driven by fear that it will not have enough acorns to survive, the squirrel neglects its current needs and holds onto the hope that it will be better off when winter comes. Other animals in the forest offer to trade acorns for knowledge about alternative food sources or den insulation but the squirrel views their queries with doubt and mistrust. As time goes on, the squirrel passes up eating acorn after acorn, until finally its strength fades and health subsides. Feeling this decline, the squirrel tries to push through to the last day of harvest but in its weakened mental and physical state the squirrel exposes himself to peril. As fate would have it, a hungry coyote came looking for food and without the energy to out run or out think the predator, the squirrel becomes prey.

What the squirrel in this story does not understand is how utilizing some of its resources in the short term is necessary to meeting its long term objective. Also, how simply trading a few acorns to other animals for knowledge about alternative food sources or how insulating its den could have made it better prepared for a change in season and possibly reduced his workload. Instead, the squirrel focused on its future fears and created a vulnerability that caused it to fail.

That is how life felt in my household. We were always denying the now for the hope of a better tomorrow. We never saw the value in learning and growing; our focus was hunkering down and storing whatever we could get. Furthermore, it was unthinkable to hand over our scant collection of acorns for an idea or piece of knowledge. Because of these ideals, the better future never came and in our weakened mental state, we were easy prey for any one of life's challenges. As time has gone on, I have learned that what I prepare for and expect usually occurs. Growing up we prepared for and expected hardships and they came. Now I try to focus my energy on preparing for abundance and breakthroughs, and guess what, they have come.

If you're a dreamer like me, it's hard to create a vision in that environment. Every day, week and month your focus is spent on keeping water out of the boat, as opposed to looking for a new boat. My surrounding relationships did not push me and the people around me did not reach for significance in life. They did not understand swinging for the fences when getting on base was their objective. This mentality shaped my life's vision and led me to set an ultimate life achievement of owning a $100,000 home.

Fast forward to my first few years in the Air Force and

my perspective began to change. I was finally surrounded by driven people who had college degrees, life plans and visions on how to get there. At the time, I was still clipping coupons, trying to save my way to that $100,000 dream. Conversely, these people were talking about revenue streams, starting businesses and growing in their careers. As I got to know them better, I started to develop a very different vision for my life. I watched people I was smarter and more driven than, exceed my $100,000 dream with little to no effort. I saw low performers bragging about their college degrees. I saw other guys just like me working toward goals I never contemplated. My environment changed and my vision with it. Next thing you know, I was investing money, knocking out two college degrees and developing goals that previously seemed unattainable.

Jumping ahead another decade, my vision continued to grow. At this point, I had coworkers starting businesses, independently wealthy friends and acquaintances with audacious goals. That was when I started to realize how impactful the people around me were. As I began talking with these successful people, I once again started seeing a new vision for my life. This one was not confined by limited possibilities but instead existed in a world that gave me the freedom to be anything I wanted. This mindset accelerated as I sought out consistently better and more beneficial relationships. As far as I am concerned, nothing else has done more to change my perspective.

Now, I don't believe there are any limits on my dreams. In a lower middle class neighborhood, no one grows up wanting to be a professional mentor or motivational speaker, yet now that is my passion. It's a different world when you change your surroundings and start interacting with people that push you. So my advice is to develop an inner circle of people that challenge your intelligence, drive you toward success and lift up those around them. These are the people who can help you create a vision for your life and assist you in reaching your potential.

Hitch yourself to the right wagons

If you want to increase your chances of being successful, make sure you are in the right relationships. I would start by making sure you are in the right romantic one. As a member of the military, I have seen how being in the wrong romantic relationship can create chaos and strife for driven people. If you are looking for that person, here are some things to look for.

First, find a person who is committed to battling and staying in the trenches with you. This will make the valleys of life much more bearable.

Second, find someone who can unselfishly celebrate your successes. People who try to take credit for others achievements are often lacking fulfillment in their own lives.

Third, look for someone that makes you feel confident in who you are and in your God given abilities. None of us are perfect but we are all perfect for someone.

Fourth, choose someone that builds you up when the rest of the world tries to tear you down. A quote I feel summarizes this point came from Miranda Lambert when she was married to Blake Shelton. Media outlets were reporting that she was getting fat and here's how Blake responded. *"Miranda asked Blake, 'Dude, why didn't you tell me I got fat?' Blake said, 'It is not my job to tell you you're fat. It is my job to tell you you're beautiful."* To me, Blake chose to build her up when the media tried to tear her down. Being that light in the darkness is so important when your person is taking a hit.

Fifth, find someone you can be vulnerable with, without feeling weak. It's hard to give someone your heart if you think they'll damage it.

Sixth, pick someone who will hold you accountable when life starts throwing obstacles your way. Sometimes the best way to love someone is to tell them to get their rear in gear!

Seventh, find someone you can develop joint goals with. I have made the mistake of setting goals with past partners and realizing down the line that they were not bought in. This made me feel like I was pulling the train alone.

You may be the pilot of your life but I recommend finding a good navigator to help keep your journey on course.

Choosing appropriate friends is also incredibly important. Friends are the people you bounce life off of. You can ask for their opinion and get a truthful, unfiltered response back. As Proverbs 27:6 states, *"Wounds from a friend can be trusted, but an enemy multiplies kisses."* With true friends, you don't question their underlying intentions or actions; they say and do things for you because they care. Friends care about your relationships, career and goals. They can check you when you start heading down the wrong path and bolster your resolve when you get weary. Close or far, when you have a true friend you know you are never alone. Having a suitable, consistent friend core will help keep you on track and help you avoid foreseeable mistakes.

Finally, finding the right mentor can change your life. But what if you haven't found the right one yet? I would suggest looking for someone that is about ten years ahead of where you want to be. I chose this timeframe because it usually produces people who are still current in the areas of your interests but have navigated the furor of the voyage. This key person should provide ideas based on where you are headed, pitfalls to avoid along the way and illustrate a relatively recent path to success. Don't be afraid to ask these people the hard questions. Ensure your intent in the relationship is clear and don't overstep boundaries. If they give you advice, either listen and enact or go find another mentor. Nothing sours this relationship more than the feeling of wasted time.

Many people confuse a mentor with a friend. They are not necessarily the same. Do not look for a mentor who is always trying to make you feel good about yourself. Instead, find someone who will give it to you straight and directs you to leave your comfort zone. If you are looking for a friend then find one, but a mentor is meant to guide you, push you and help you achieve your goals. Their role is to bring out your true potential and reveal hidden talents within. Of course, you may transition to a friendship at a certain point but don't get familiar to soon.

Finally, remain open to having multiple mentors because every new perspective assists in your growth.

Consistency in your habits

"The best way to predict your future is to create it." - *Abraham Lincoln*

Consistent habits create the framework for success. They provide structure for your life so you can build toward your dreams. How many successful people do you know who lack consistent habits? I can't think of any! However, I can name a lot of people who have achieved mediocrity by doing whatever, whenever.

As I stated at the end of chapter two about forging a sword, consistent hammering and working of the metal is what makes a sword. It is not the fire or the plan that gives a sword its shape. Those two elements only aid in the effectiveness of the hammering. It is the focused consistency of each strike and determination of its creator that shapes the metal into something worthwhile. So if you are looking to make something of yourself, you need to figure out where you need consistent habits in your life.

I see consistent habits like a wooden match chain reaction. If you haven't seen one of these videos yet, I highly recommend you go watch one. It's basically match sticks set up to catch fire, kind of like dominos falling. To start the chain reaction, you need to either light your own match or stand close enough to a fire that lights it for you. After the first match is lit, you must keep the fire going. This is where the spacing between matches matter. In your habits, you must maintain consistent spacing between your actions. If you are inconsistent, the match will burn out and you will fail to keep the flame alive. If you have too much space between your actions, your lit match will have to burn hotter or fall forward to light the next one. However, if you establish good, consistent habits, you will feed the next match and the next one, until you finally reach your goal. If your matches are really close together, like high consistency in your habits, your fire will burn even hotter. And if you're burning hot enough and other peoples matches get close, you might even start a chain reaction in another person's life.

For me to complete this book, I had to be consistent in the management of my time. Between work, family and recharging, I had to seek ways to use my leisure time wisely. As I searched for squandered minutes in the day, I came to realize that I needed to remove unproductive distractions such as television and social media from my life. Additionally, I had to consistently rise early to write before the kids got up and the chaos ensued. Both were challenging for me, but I believe this book and effort I gave will do more to impact the lives of others than watching another football game or liking another post would have.

So what are your habits creating?

Consistent leadership

"When the leader is morally weak and his discipline not strict, when his instructions and guidance are not enlightened, when there are no consistent rules, neighboring rulers will take advantage of this." -Sun Tzu

To be a good leader, I believe at a minimum you need to be competent, caring and consistent. On one of my deployments, I had a Crew Commander that never took the time to understand his leadership philosophy or understand how to best support his people and their ambitions. Instead, he tried to be all things to all people. At times while I executed the mission, he told me, *"Go take a break, you're working too hard"* or *"Why don't you go watch a movie?"* In response I would reply with something like, *"No thanks, Sir! If I'm going to be away from my family, I'm going to work hard and make sure the time I spend here counts for something."*

I know this probably bothered him but it was clear he didn't take pride in his work. When he left for hours, I took the liberty to push the mission forward. When I didn't comply with his direction to take it easy, he would become guilt stricken and try to do more stuff around the work center. That is when he would get "involved" and start asking me questions about mission related stuff, how equipment functioned, how the *"buttonology"* worked, etc... In his position, this knowledge was completely unnecessary and if he really cared about this stuff he could have paid attention like the rest of us when we went through training.

To make matters worse, his uncertain leadership style caused him to change philosophies on what seemed like a daily basis. From what I could gather, at least once a week he would write friends and ask how he should lead our team. Based on the chaos we endured, it appeared as if every person gave him different advice. One day he would come in overly optimistic and want to learn about everything. The next day he would bark orders and expect to be looped in on everything. A day later he would want to know the depths of our souls and start up some crazy philosophical conversation. Luckily, by day four his authentic leadership style would resurface and he would leave for hours or go around telling us to watch movies.

From my perspective as a subordinate, this is the worst kind of leadership to experience. I believe subordinates need consistent behavior from their leaders so they can adapt to their leaders specific style. As a subordinate, I don't really care if you want to be a jerk; all I ask is that you be a jerk every day so I can tailor my messaging, actions and interactions to meet you where you are. If you want to be involved, be involved! If you're a nice competent person, that's fantastic! Just do your best to stay consistent so the people around you can operate in the environment you create.

Consistent mindset

"A positive thinker sees the invisible, feels the intangible and achieves the impossible." -Unknown

How do you view yourself? Are you deserving, intelligent or capable enough to get what you want out of life? How do you view the world? Do you see it as a place full of possibilities or full of risks to be avoided? To reach your definition of success, the mindset you have about yourself and the world around you matters.

Growing up without money taught me some survival skills I've had to unlearn. For years I avoided risk, kept my head down and executed my job in an attempt to ensure security in my finances. Watching my Dad get laid off showed me how quickly you can go from living comfortably to not making ends meet. Because of the panic caused by this impactful event, I sought security before all else. Now I dismiss this mindset and reach for true fulfillment because neither you nor I were made to live in fear.

Another poor person habit I've had to unlearn is being frugal. Now don't get me wrong, I still use coupons and discounts but the kind of penny pinching I am talking about has undoubtedly kept me from personal and professional growth. Walter Bond, a great motivational speaker says in one of his speeches, *"Take your money and get information and access and you will get good habits and will get good rituals and you will go to the next level!"* However, this statement is lost on someone watching every penny and valuing $20 in their savings account over a potentially life changing piece of information garnered from a book or seminar. Now I recognize that information has value and the more I take in, the more capable I become.

For me, it's still a struggle to spend money on items outside of my categories of necessity. Yet, as I have opened up my world to new people, information and ideas, I have changed my short sighted views to see a world full of options. I do not focus on the challenges of my efforts but on the possibilities they hold. I do not focus on the hundreds of dollars I can save but on the thousands I can make. I am capable and so are you! So get started, keep speaking life into you actions and you will achieve what you set out to do.

Question 1: What surroundings have you chosen?

Question 2: Who is your wagon hitched too?

Question 3: What habits have you established to keep your flame going?

Question 4: Do you know your leadership style? Do your people? What is it?

Question 5: What mindset have you chosen? Why?

LIVE IN CHARGE

"The only impossible journey is the one you never begin." -Tony Robbins

This is my call to action for you. How do you live? Do you react to life or do you live in charge? Will you take back your 1% and change your life? Will you make changes in your professional life with these new perspectives or just go back to the same predictable life you've always lived?

What's taking you to the next level?

"The secret of getting ahead is getting started." -Mark Twain

Have you ever been standing, waiting for an elevator that seemed to never come? I have and one day I realized that instead of standing motionless, waiting for something else to take me to the next level, I could take myself. Now I know this may not seem like an Aha moment, but hear me out.

How often are you waiting for something to take you to the next level in life? Are you waiting for someone to leave their position so you can get a shot at it? Well, what if they choose someone else and your waiting was wasted. Are you waiting for the right time to pursue your passion? Well, if you're looking for reasons to not start, you'll always find one.

If you want to move up in life, something has to take you there. Either you can apathetically wait for an elevator or you can choose to start climbing the stairs.

When you wait for an elevator, you become dependent on a number of factors. First, once you press the button you have to wait for the elevator to complete its other tasks before it comes to you. Second, since an elevator is made up of moving parts, you'll need to trust that someone else did their job so you can get where you want. Third, you have to hope that someone hasn't pressed every button on the panel, impeding your progress along the way. Fourth, what happens if the elevator breaks or the power goes out? You get stuck! How do you reach your destination when your only option fails? Fifth, what if the elevator you're waiting for is not strong enough to pull you up? Not all elevators are created equal and every single one has a limit.

By taking an elevator to the next level, you need things outside of your control to go right and an external energy source to get you there.

Conversely, taking the stairs puts you in charge. When you take the stairs, you don't wait for something to come get you. You take yourself! With every step, you will be heading in the right direction, up! Taking the stairs requires you to engage your muscles and in return you will become stronger. If something happens along the way, you can exit at any floor and find another path to keep climbing. Additionally, when you take the stairs you're almost guaranteed to reach your destination because you've avoided the risk of breakdowns along the way. Finally, if the level you want to reach requires an elevator ride at some point, climbing the stairs will put you closer to your final destination.

The effects of being passive are massive, so take charge of your upward momentum and step up to the next level.

Lead from your position

"The key to successful leadership today is influence, not authority." -Kenneth Blanchard

I once had a person come into my office right before a deployment and express his concerns about going down range with a challenging person who outranked him. He believed that because this person had authority over him, he was at the mercy of any order or idea he wanted executed. After he expressed his dismay, I asked him, *"So what can you do about this situation?"* To which he replied, *"Be respectful and do my best at whatever he tells me to do."* In response, I told him that giving respect was right but that he should seek to influence and even respectfully challenge ideas that could prove detrimental to the mission.

Since their team was small, chasing ideas down a rabbit hole could have a significant impact on their effectiveness. I told him to lead from the position he's in. Learn how the people on his crew worked and find out how to successfully communicate with them. Also, find out what this difficult person is receptive to and tailor your approach to present ideas that benefit the team. Understand that you may not get credit but have solace in knowing that your contributions led to overall positive outcomes. Take actions at your level to effect the changes you want. Don't be reckless but once you understand the mission and figure out what level of risk the people around you are willing to take, step out and try something different. Know your "Why" for pushing the envelope and avoid doing things for selfish reasons. A purpose propels progression! Understand how your actions impact your team or the customers you support. And when you have success, share it with people and use it to build momentum for your team and mission.

Furthermore, something I hear too often from people in leadership positions is that there are no leaders in their organization. These people seem to be looking for someone externally to lead them. Well guess what, you're a leader. Don't complain about needing a leader, be a leader. Maybe God put you there to be the leader and for some reason you're looking around for someone else. Are you waiting for the people who you say aren't leading to give you permission to lead? If so, why? If they aren't leading then chances are they won't get in your way. If you see a leadership need in your organization, fill it. Be the person that breaks the trend or someday your subordinates will be saying the same things about you.

Sometimes the people with leadership abilities on a team aren't in a position of authority. Does that mean that they can't lead? No, of course not! All they need to do is change their approach. Being a leader requires you to move those above and below you in a positive direction. It requires you to understand the people around you, the skillset you possess and figuring out how to help steer the team to success. Stop worrying about the position you're in and focus on position you want your team to be in.

Start by maintaining a positive attitude and ensuring there is clear communication throughout the team. Use tact and respect when turbulence hits. Initiate new ideas and have disagreements in private, so those in the position of authority don't feel challenged in a group environment. Also, keep your focus on the outcomes and ensure the details are being executed. Finally, lead in your own genuine way. People can always sniff out a phony. If you do these things, you can be an effective leader in any position.

When your destination is in Canada, start walking north

"Ask yourself if what you're doing today is getting you closer to where you want to be tomorrow." -Unknown

What should you do when you have an idea, goal or plan that doesn't have a clear ending? Start walking! So often in life we have a general sense of where we want to go but when the time comes to move on it, we get bogged down with planning or wanting clearer direction. I've seen this occur at work on several occasions. We get told to revector or things are changing, yet we wait and wait to take action. *"Standby to standby"* is the best saying I know to capture this active inaction. But what if we started taking some steps in the right direction when we're given a new heading? What if when we're told our destination is in Canada, we just started walking north?

To illustrate this example, let's say your boss told you that you had to walk to some unknown city in Canada. What would you do? Would you start planning for every contingency along the way? Would you convince yourself that you need more equipment than is truly necessary? Would you stay put until they told you exactly what city, street and building you need to go too? Or would you just start heading north?

For some, the process of making a decision is harder than the challenges they'll face along the way. My belief is that you should grab the necessities and start walking. As you head in the right direction you will find things start opening up for you. The vision will become clearer and the details will work themselves out. When others see you traverse this uncertain terrain, they may join you on your journey. There is something about a person or team that takes decisive action and builds momentum. It's like they become magnets attracting the right people. If you stay put and wait for precise direction, you'll probably keep finding excuses for not moving out. *"We don't have all the equipment we need, we're not properly resourced, we don't have enough people for this journey, etc..."* But how can you validate these concerns if you never start the journey and figure out what the critical needs are? And worst case scenario, if you find that you're missing something critical, stop in a store along the way and pick it up. This is what we do when we're out and about, traveling, or heading to the campsite, right? Whatever your need is, it's probably not exclusive to your launch point and chances are you can probably find whatever it is once underway.

So, if you want to be an author, start writing every day. You don't have to know the book title, table of contents or have a publisher to get started. All you have to do is start writing and those things will emerge.

If you want to get in shape, start doing workouts that appeal to you. You don't need perfect form, all the clothes or to know all the terms to get started. All you have to do is get active and your progress will create momentum.

If you want to start eating healthy, start incorporating more fruits and veggies into your diet. Once you start feeling better and develop a taste for healthier food, you'll start looking for recipes that match your preferences. Then when your recipes and go-to meals change to healthier options, you will be on your way to a sustainable healthy lifestyle.

Progress stops where effort ends! So when you have a direction for your goal, head out. Sitting around waiting for the right moment is a waste of your time. Trying to plan for every obstacle creates a never ending loop. When you are told your destination is in Canada, start walking north! Eventually you will find out whether you are supposed to go to Toronto or Vancouver. Either way, chances are that you will be closer to your final destination if you just get moving.

Leading your interactions

"You can get everything in life you want if you will just help enough other people get what they want." -Zig Ziglar

For two years I worked as a server at Cracker Barrel. If you aren't familiar with this restaurant chain, they are typically right off the highway and cater heavily to travelers passing through. Their basic tenets are to offer quality meals in an old timey environment with an emphasis on value. Because of this mostly transient clientele and focus on value, the environment Cracker Barrel creates doesn't usually generate large tips for their servers. Therefore, if you want to make a living at this job, you must concentrate on turnover rate and finding unique ways to create pleasant customer experiences. The key to achieving these two essential objectives is to confidently and efficiently lead the interactions with your customers.

To give you an idea of how I lead my interactions, I will walk you through a scenario.

As I walked up to a table, I looked for clues to determine if they were local, from out of town or have been traveling. The most obvious indications are T-shirts or hats with tourist destinations and collegiate or sports team apparel. A less obvious clue would be folks who were stretching or moving more than normal due to their long car rides. I then used this information to build our initial connection. After a friendly greeting, I would ask a tailored question like, *"How'd you like Yellowstone?"* if they are wearing a Yellowstone National Park shirt. *"What's your connection to Texas Tech?"* if they were wearing a Red Raiders shirt or *"How are the Cardinals doing this year?"* if they were sporting an Arizona Cardinal hat. If they looked squirmy, I would simply ask *"Are y'all heading anywhere today?"* Everyone one of these questions created conversations of interest to them.

Once I established a little rapport, it was time to determine their needs and figure out how to best position myself for a solid tip. If they were traveling, I would say something to the effect of, *"We'll if y'all are looking to get back on the road, our meatloaf and chicken and dumplings come out of the kitchen quickly and if you pair it with green beans and mashed potatoes, we can get you a good meal and back on the road before you know it. I'll even make sure to send you off with a cup of sweet tea to make sure you feel like you got your money's worth."* This approach catered to their needs and helped me turn a table quickly.

If they weren't in a hurry, I would try to push more expensive products and give them a bit more attention. Point blank, if they were going to occupy my table for a longer period of time I needed a bigger tip and my best shot at that was to have a higher bill. Also, since our interactions were going to be longer, I had to ensure their drinks stayed full; even if that meant bringing new ones before their old ones were finished. This kept me in the driver's seat of our interactions and gave them the impression that I was being attentive. Additionally, it was a quick touch point with a nearly perfect record of positive contact.

If they were local, I poured on the local charm and tried to build some camaraderie to establish a regular customer. For this, I did my best to remember unique characteristics about them, asked their name and tried to memorize their order so I could add a personal touch throughout. Planting these seeds was especially helpful during the slow times when you got by name requested and were able to keep your section filled while others only had one or two tables occupied in their section.

Sometimes you would get folks that weren't worth your time. They would complain about small things, keep talking when you tried to break away or specifically ask about the least expensive items on the menu. Of course, I still treated them well but I recognized that they were not an efficient use of my time. In response, I gave them the minimum amount of effort required to close out the transaction and get them on their way. It was nothing personal, but sometimes a person's needs and yours don't align, so you need to move on. After all, you have to make a living and time is money in every industry.

Finally, by helping enough people get what they wanted, such as getting back on the road or showing that you cared, I got what I wanted, like higher tips and a loyal customer base. An added bonus with this intentional approach was that it helped my boss as well. The more money I made, the more money the store made. In turn, this outcome opened me up to advancement opportunities. Furthermore, since my actions helped management meet its goals, I was certainly in their favor. Throughout my working life, nothing has helped me advance quicker than helping my managers meet their goals or finding ways to make their job easier.

Now that you know my approach, how can you live in charge of your interactions at work? How can you quickly establish rapport, find ways to interact in mutually beneficial ways and efficiently move past unproductive engagements?

Take charge of the complainers

"Complainers change their complaints, but they never reduce the amount of time spent in complaining." -Mason Cooley

Have you ever known somebody who complained nonstop at work? This process is broken, that system is frustrating, and so on. Yet these same people take zero constructive steps to fix the problems they see. How should you handle this? How do you take charge of their attitude?

My first two questions in these situations are;

1. What's the intent of your complaint?

2. What have you done to fix it?

The first question is often greeted with a blank stare because sometimes they realize there is no real intent other than to complain. On occasion you'll get someone who genuinely wants to fix the issue but doesn't know where to start. And every once in a while, you will have a person who is just deeply frustrated and needs to vent. Two of three instances are fine in small doses but they should be handled in an appropriate setting with the correct peer group.

If someone is just complaining, especially in a group of varying ranks, positions or responsibilities, pull them aside and get to the root of the issue. This is a bad look on them and their team. Letting this behavior persist will negatively affect the people around them, give the impression that working with them is laborious and make your job as a leader more difficult.

If someone is simply expressing their frustrations, ask what they've done to try and fix the problem. If they have exhausted their options, look for training, experts or resources to help them overcome their challenges. If they are vocalizing this in a group setting, maybe ask the group if this is an issue for them as well. If it is, I would apply the same training, experts or resources solution across the team to help them overcome these challenges as well. The key is to take over the conversation when the frustrations start and keep the focus on finding solutions, as opposed to letting the environment become toxic.

If a person just needs to vent, pull them into a private location and let them air their grievances. Never complain to people below your position and always be someone your subordinates feel comfortable talking with. Keep an open mind and closed mouth until they finish their comments. Realize that some people aren't looking for solutions; they just want to vent and get back to working the issue on their own. This behavior is okay, as long as they aren't going around spreading negativity.

In the military, I expect new people to complain. In fact, I have no problem with first term Airman complaining about things. In my opinion, they were not aware of all the issues they would experience when they joined and they typically haven't yet developed the necessary coping skills to deal with their frustrations. In these cases, I try to remind them that the benefits outweigh the aggravations and to stay focused on the positives that come from joining the service.

When some reenlists, my tolerance for this behavior decreases. At this point, they know what they are dealing with and have willfully chosen to remain in the environment.

After a second reenlistment, I have zero tolerance for unproductive complaining. At this point anyone who stays in knows exactly what they signed up for and should understand how to handle themselves. If they didn't want to deal with the known frustrations that come with being in the military, they had two chances to walk away and do something else. At this point, the complaining stops! If you need to vent, go do it in the appropriate places with the appropriate people. Complaining in front of lower ranking individuals is not keeping it real or just being honest, it's poisonous. If you don't like something, work to fix it or leave! You need the military more than it needs you. And if being in the military is no longer a good fit for you, go somewhere else and do something else. Being miserable everyday isn't good for you or the military, so go find something that makes you happy.

Raise your game or take a seat

I love self-starters! To me, there is something special about a person who steps up to the plate, tackles an issue, makes personal sacrifices for the team or finds a way to get a job done. But how do you handle someone who regularly bites off more than they can chew? You know, the person who seeks glory but doesn't want to put in the hard work that comes with it! I believe a person like this needs a leader with the courage and tact to speak truth into their habits, actions and mindset.

The big stage comes with more responsibility than most people realize. When you stand in front of a bigwig you not only represent yourself, you also represent your team. That means if your etiquette isn't squared away or skills aren't polished, you reflect poorly on your team. The expectation changes when you take a lead position. How you handle tough questions and unencumbered criticism matters. Little things such as decorum and professional intangibles matter. The limelight exposes bad habits and blind spots so if you want the center stage, be prepared to have your weaknesses exposed.

Additionally, if you want to play in the big leagues, here are a few things you might need to hear. Successful organizations are built like a team and teams are built to win. Therefore, you should expect team leaders to play the people who give them the best chance to win. Is that you? Have you developed your skills to succeed on the field or are you just talking a big game from the bench? What evidence does your leadership team have to reevaluate your position?

If you want to be a major league player, you need to let go of your minor league habits. Become a student, listen to your coaches and develop the skills needed for the big stage. Develop thick skin and prepare yourself to play hard ball. Professionals accept the challenges in front of them, so if you want to be major league player stop asking for minor league pitching! Put in the work, develop your skills, accept feedback, be adaptable and raise your game to attain new levels of success.

Live in Charge of each day

"Each day comes bearing its own gifts. Untie the ribbons."-Ruth Schabaker

How do you start your day? Is it a mad scramble after waking up late only to feel rushed running from one thing to the next? If so, you're not in living in charge of the day. You're just reacting! But what if you could live in charge of your day? What would that even look like for you? Here's a few ways I took charge of my days and significantly improved my productivity and mental state.

First, wake up early. I wake up about two hours before I leave for work. This allows me to read some scriptures, eat a healthy breakfast, drink some coffee, work on goals, get my kids fed, dressed and get out of the door without operating in a panicked state. For some, a morning workout does wonders for their daily mindset. Just remember, this habit starts the night before by going to bed at a decent hour.

Second, start your day on a positive note. I start my day by reading scriptures before work and listening to motivational speeches in the car on my commute. These two habits mentally prepare me for the challenges I face throughout the day. Additionally, I often find that I can apply something I have learned that morning to a scenario I encounter later in the day.

To start my kids off on a positive note, I ask them two simple questions each morning before dropping them off at school. *"Whose day is it?"* to which they respond *"My day!"* Followed by, *"And what are you going to do today?"* to which they respond *"Learn something new!"* This simple ritual gives them a sense of ownership over the day and keeps them curious to learn and grow.

Third, spend some time in gratitude each morning. If you have a job, are driving a car or move around without pain, you have something to be grateful for. Being thankful for small blessings puts you in a forward thinking position. If you don't have these things, take action to change your condition. Take note of the positives in your life, be thankful for the opportunities life has given you and capitalize on them to take your life where you want it to go.

Take away

What I want to say more than anything in this chapter is, *"Don't be the greatest person that never lived!"* If you have the ability to do incredible things, take charge of your life and do it. Anything less is a waste of your God given talents and a disservice to those around you.

Question 1: What's taking you to the next level in life?

Question 2: How can you lead with influence from your position at work?

Question 3: How can you move closer to your destination?

Question 4: How can you lead interactions in your personal and professional life?

Question 5: What are some ways you can take charge of complainers in your life?

Question 6: How can you take charge of each day?

CONCLUSION

I strongly believe that as humans we experience things to help us draw closer to each other. Suffering connects people who have little in common. Unexpected inspiration provides a much needed spark in someone's life. Kindness builds communities and we learn from those around us. Additionally, we all have something to teach and can all contribute to the success of others. Our joy, pain, experiences and perspectives are the raw materials we've built our lives with, so don't let them go to waste. Share your story as I have in this book. Talk about your journey and help others navigate life. Make a connection with people and build unbreakable bonds. Connection makes us human and our personal stories are the glue.

Also, if you're unhappy in life, please don't accept things the way they are. If you don't like something, change it. If you want something different, pursue it. Embrace who you are, find your God given talents and make a difference in the world. As George Bernard Shaw says, *"The reasonable man adapts himself to the world; the unreasonable one persists in trying to adapt the world to himself. Therefore all progress depends on the unreasonable man."*

You were not put on this earth to live a mediocre life. You were meant to improve it one person at a time. So find out how and start living.

Finally, thank you so much for reading The Paperback Mentor. I sincerely hope you have found a new perspective to apply in your life. And if you connected with my story, please reach out and let me know. If I can positively affect the life of one person, this year of writing will have been worth it.

ThePaperbackMentor@gmail.com

God bless you and be well.

Made in the USA
Monee, IL
07 September 2020

41626691R00121